Sea Kayaking
the Gulf
Islands

Mary Ann Snowden

To all who play a part, however small,
in protecting these coastal waterways.

Rocky
Mountain Books
Calgary–Victoria–Vancouver

Front cover: Paddling in Trincomali Channel west of Porlier pass. Photo: Paul Davidson.

We acknowledge the financial support of the Government of Canada through the Book Publishing Industry Development Program (BPIDP) and the support of the Alberta Foundation for the Arts for our publishing program.

Copyright © 2004 Mary Ann Snowden

Printed in Canada

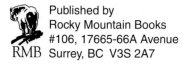 Published by
Rocky Mountain Books
#106, 17665-66A Avenue
RMB   Surrey, BC V3S 2A7

National Library of Canada Cataloguing in Publication

Snowden, Mary Ann, 1953-
     Sea kayak the Gulf Islands / Mary Ann Snowden.

Includes index.
ISBN 1-894765-51-6

     1. Sea kayaking--British Columbia--Gulf Islands--Guidebooks. 2. Gulf Islands (B.C.)--Guidebooks. I. Title.

GV776.15.B7S665 2004   797.1'224'0971128   C2004-900730-0

New   16.95

Contents

Acknowledgements

There are many people to whom I owe my sincere thanks.

First is Meredith Reeve at Parks Canada Gulf Islands National Park Reserve. She answered my many questions about the new Park Reserve and on top of everything else that she does she agreed to review those parts of my text relevant to the park. For helping me to get it right my sincere thanks to her.

For providing information on the newest of the BC Marine Parks, Wakes Cove, my thanks to Drew Chapman.

A sincere thanks for photos and for their rescuing me from digital imagery ignorance to Kelli Irving, David Spittlehouse and Sherry Kirkvold. Dave Pinel, Bruce Holland and Maurice Robinson – my thanks for prints and slides. And a special thanks to Andrew Madding for his many images and to Bob Davidson who not only provided images but who asked, "where would you like me to paddle next?"

As the new Gulf Islands National Park Reserve has a significant presence on Saturna Island a good part of the research for this revision was focused on this island. My thanks to several Saturna residents for their insights, most notably Bob and Bev Bruce, of Saturna Sea Kayaking. And to CRD park caretaker, Ray Barrow, who kept an eye out for me as I undertook a solo in April off East Point.

A special thanks to Dave Pinel who reminded me that all paddlers can play an important role, however small, in conserving these incredible waterways. And subsequently my thanks to both Alan Wilson and Laurie MacBride for their commitment to bringing conservation issues to the attention of the paddling community.

And finally my thanks to Heritage House. Most notably to Vivian Sinclair who made me feel so welcome. To Rodger Touche for his interest in this and future books and to Tony Daffern for the production and layout of this book.

Disclaimer

There are inherent risks in sea kayaking. While the author has done her best to provide accurate information and to point out potential hazards, conditions may change owing to weather and other factors. It is up to the users of this guide to learn the necessary skills for safe paddling and to exercise caution in potentially hazardous areas. Please read the introduction to this book and, in particular study the Trip Rating guidelines on pages 8 and 9.

Paddlers using this book do so entirely at their own risk and the author and publishers disclaim any liability for injury or other damage that may be sustained by anyone using the access and/or paddling routes described.

The Gulf Islands

Huddled around the southern tip of Vancouver Island within the waters of eastern Juan de Fuca, Haro Strait and the southern Strait of Georgia lies a dozen large islands and hundreds of smaller islets collectively referred to as the Gulf Islands. For years the waterways between these islands have attracted countless boaters. Spectacular scenery, low rainfall and the many protected waterways are among the features that add to the small boating appeal. These same attributes offer ideal paddling conditions for the sea kayaker and canoeist.

Hundreds of kilometres of shoreline offer countless hours of intertidal exploration, while the open water yields the privileged traveller a glimpse of the majestic orca whale or the elusive harbour porpoise. Quiet coves, pebble beaches and sandy shores allow for putting ashore, exploring inland, setting up camp or for simply gazing to seaward.

Those who have paddled these waters for decades never weary of this sheltered seascape. The secluded beach visited many times looks different with a change in the tide, season, weather or the light. Those who paddle these waters for the first time are bound to be taken in—so much so that they too will want to return.

The Gulf Islands and eastern Juan de Fuca waters are sheltered from the extreme weather associated with Vancouver Island's west coast. Winds, especially during the summer months, are often calm, and the climate is relatively dry. Open water distances are short; it is rare that a paddler will travel more than three miles before discovering another shore. Strong currents are perhaps the greatest hazard, yet most are predictable and in most instances avoidable.

The shoreline is not only stunningly beautiful but rich in variety. Eroded sandstone cliffs, precipitous bluffs, sand–fringed lagoons and countless tiny islets are all part of the paddling experience. Onshore are historically interesting features: shell middens dating back five thousand years, a turn–of–the–century saltery and the crumbling remains of a leper colony.

The wildlife is as rich and as varied as the landscape. Within the paddler's touching distance are the colourful creatures that occupy the intertidal zone flowery plumose anemones, ochre stars, spiny red urchins, limpets and chitons, green anemones and both the California and blue mussels.

Attracted to an abundant food supply are several marine mammals, among them the mink and raccoon that rummage through the kelp for crab. Offshore, harbour seals curiously eye intruders while the river otters frolic with boundless energy. California and Steller sea lions return to these waters each winter and are most often seen by the off–season paddlers either basking on rocky islets or bobbing in the current. The most breathtaking sight is the breaking of the waters by a pod of orca. Although sightings are infrequent, viewing these magnificent whales only metres away is truly an awe–inspiring experience.

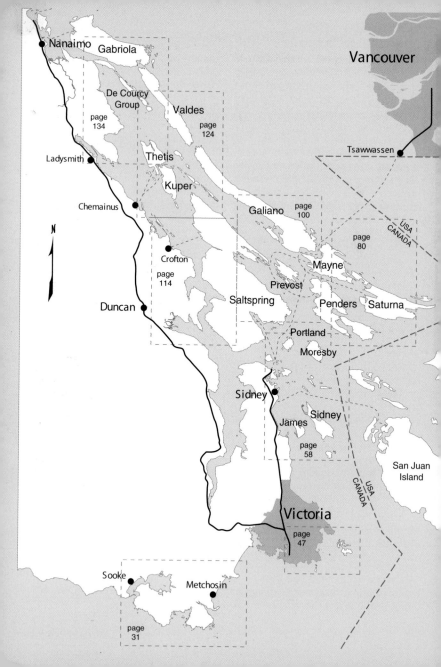

Vancouver

Nanaimo

Gabriola

De Courcy
Group

page
134

Valdes

page
124

Ladysmith

Thetis

Tsawwassen

Kuper

Chemainus

Galiano

page
100

USA
CANADA

N

Crofton

page
80

page
114

Mayne

Prevost

Duncan

Saltspring

Penders

Saturna

Portland

Moresby

Sidney

Sidney

James

page
58

San Juan
Island

USA
CANADA

Victoria

page
47

Sooke

Metchosin

page
31

grass shallows, watching for fish to come within striking distance. Flocks of glaucous–winged gulls scream overhead. Onshore, black oystercatchers chisel away at the mussels exposed at low tide, while the belted kingfisher searches for fish from an elevated perch.

In contrast to the lush rain forest occurring along most of the Pacific coast, dry woodlands are found throughout the Gulf Islands. The area receives a mere 80 cm (32 in) of rain a year. (Prickly pears, found on many of the southern islands, grow in testimony to this dryness.) Douglas fir still dominate the landscape, although many have been logged because of their high commercial value. Frequently associated with the towering firs is the arbutus, Canada's only broadleafed evergreen. Recognizable by its coppery bark and gnarled trunk, this tree prefers sunny locations, especially on bluffs overlooking the sea. Along with the arbutus is the Garry oak, BC's only native oak. Although the tree has been depleted by encroaching urbanization, paddlers will still see this gnarled and twisted species growing throughout the islands.

It would be unforgivable to not mention the wildflowers blossoming throughout these dry woodlands in spring. Peak blooming occurs in April and May when the meadows are ablaze with yellow monkey–flowers, blue camas, pink sea–blush, chocolate and white lilies, blue–eyed Mary and the lemon–coloured bloom of the Oregon grape.

Protected waterways and low rainfall adds to the appeal of this area. Photo: Dave Pinel.

Thousands of migratory birds grace the skies and waters around the islands, significantly adding to the appeal of winter paddling. Not all birds are seasonal visitors—throughout the year paddlers can expect to see any number of species that are permanent residents. Most impressive is the bald eagle; the white–headed master. The jet black pelagic and double–crested cormorants, often found close to their cliff–ledge nesting sites, are a common sight. Meanwhile, spindly–legged great blue herons wade through the eel

Trip Rating

Routes described in this guide have been rated according to the paddling skills required, normal sea and shoreline conditions and the level of risk normally associated with such conditions. The rating given to a trip is an indication of what to expect in good, summer conditions. It is an assessment of risk, taking into account paddling skill level and difficulties likely to be encountered.

Difficulty is a measure of sea conditions: wind, waves, currents, tide rips and length of open–water crossings, and shoreline conditions: surf and infrequent and/or difficult landings.

Risk is the possibility of inconvenience, discomfort, injury or even loss of life. For the paddler, the level of risk is not constant. Along the same route and with the same paddling conditions, different paddlers will encounter different levels of risk. For a beginner, risky conditions may include small wavelets that arise before white–capped waves appear. For a more skilled paddler the same waves may hardly be noticeable. Risk can be reduced by good paddling skills, knowledge and judgement. Risk is increased in worsening conditions, remote locations and with poor decision–making.

There is a complex relationship between paddling skills, difficulty and risk. The individual paddler's skill level, the nature of the route, changing weather, and the presence of a competent leader are essential factors in determining the difficulty and risk of a sea kayak journey.

Sound decision–making is critical to the enjoyment and safety of sea kayaking touring and an experienced leader will often reduce difficulty and risk to acceptable levels. In the company of a skilled leader, a beginner can paddle safely along a coast rated intermediate. With good leadership a large portion of the Gulf Islands coastline is accessible to beginner–level paddlers and a coastline rated as "advanced" is by no means the sole domain of the advanced paddler.

The rating descriptions below cover many, but not all of the factors required to assess difficulty and risk. There may be other factors to be considered such as river outflows, reflected waves, the profile of a surf beach and the limitations of gear and cold water.

The skill–levels referred to below correspond to the conditions i.e. intermediate paddlers have the attributes necessary to safely travel in intermediate conditions.

Novice conditions – minimal risk
- Sheltered locations with stable conditions.
- Wind calm (less than 8 knots); sea state calm to rippled.
- Travel is along shore with abundant easy landing sites.
- Frequent opportunities for communication and road access; assistance is nearby.

Trip Rating courtesy Doug Alderson.

A group of novice paddlers can travel safely on day trips along the shore. Poor decisions or misinterpreting changing weather or sea conditions is unlikely to cause harm or significant inconvenience.

Beginner conditions – low risk
- Mostly sheltered locations with stable conditions.
- Light winds (0–11 knots) current (0–0.5 knots) Sea state calm to light chop.
- Abundant easy landing sites and short open crossings less than 1.5 nmi.
- Frequent opportunities for communication and access; assistance may be up to an hour away.

A group of beginners can travel safely on day trips. Intermediate paddlers familiar with the area could lead beginners on an overnight trip. Poor decisions or misinterpreting changing weather or sea conditions is likely to cause inconvenience but unlikely to cause harm.

Intermediate conditions – moderate risk
- A complex open water environment with the potential for moderate change in conditions.
- Moderate winds (12–19 knots); sea state moderate with wind waves near 0.5 meters; surf less than 1 meter; current less than 3 knots.
- Intermittent landing opportunities with some difficult landing sites; open water crossings less than 5 nmi.
- Communication may be interrupted; assistance may be more than one hour away.

A group of intermediate paddlers can travel safely on day trips. Advanced paddlers familiar with the area could lead intermediate paddlers on an extended overnight trip. Poor decisions or misinterpreting changing weather or sea conditions is likely to cause great inconvenience, the need for external rescue and possibly personal harm.

Advanced conditions – considerable risk
- Complex open water environment with frequently changing conditions.
- Continuous exposure to wind, swell or current.
- Strong winds (near 20 knots); sea state rough with wind waves near 1 metre; surf greater than 1 metre or tide rips greater than 3 knots are routine.
- Infrequent landing opportunities with some difficult landing sites; open water crossings greater than 5 nmi
- Remote locations where communications can be difficult or unavailable; assistance may be a day or more away.

A mix of intermediate and advanced paddlers can travel safely on day trips. On extended overnight trips all paddlers should have advanced skills. Poor decisions or misinterpreting changing weather or sea conditions is likely to cause personal harm, without the availability of prompt external rescue.

Planning Considerations

About This Guide

At the beginning of each of the routes in this guide is a "Difficulty" rating followed by a section called "Paddling Considerations." In this section the risks that paddlers might expect to encounter on a particular trip are described. They are however potential risks. They will not occur at all times, and in fact they could occur rather infrequently. However, paddlers must base their decision to paddle a particular route on their ability to cope with the worst–case scenarios. Upon reading the paddling considerations and consulting the trip rating on the previous two pages, most paddlers should be able to determine whether or not the route is suited to their ability.

Distances on the water are given in nautical miles, while those on land are in kilometres and statute miles.

Ferries

Paddlers following any of the routes described in this guide will undoubtedly board one of more than two dozen ferries that travel between the lower mainland, Vancouver Island and the Gulf Islands.

Ships depart regularly from Tsawwassen, linking paddlers from the mainland to Vancouver Island just north of Victoria at Swartz Bay. Some may choose to depart from the mainland ferry terminal that is north of Vancouver at Horseshoe Bay, thereby accessing Vancouver Island from Nanaimo's Departure Bay terminal. Paddlers living in Vancouver and heading to routes described for the north Gulf Islands will likely choose this option. In most other instances, this is the longer route.

Some ferries run directly to the Gulf Islands, departing several times daily from both Swartz Bay and Tsawwassen terminals. In the summer months ferries are heavily used and although sailings leave the larger terminals hourly there can be waits of two to three hours. To avoid the wait consider making reservations by calling the toll free number 1-888-724-5223. Out of province visitors call 604-444-2890.

For more information on schedules and reservations check the BC Ferries web site at www.bcferries.bc.ca.

It is cheaper to board without a vehicle, carrying kayaks and gear and paying foot–passenger rates plus a minimal fee for kayaks or canoes. This is not always going to be an option as some launch locations require vehicle access, but if you have a choice, walking on is the least expensive way for paddlers to travel by ferry. There is another hidden advantage to walking on—assured boarding. Three–hour vehicle lineups that occur on busy holiday weekends are best avoided, by anyone's standard.

Sailings are frequent enough to allow many of the routes described in this guide to be paddled as a day's excursion. For instance, paddlers could leave in the morning, park their car at the terminal and walk onto a ferry. By launching adjacent to the terminal and returning in the evening, again as a walk–on, you avoid additional expense.

Ferry operators are generally cooperative toward paddlers with kayaks and all their gear in tow. However, frequent trips between a waiting ferry and the terminal's parking area by those attempting to get organized may receive a different sort of response. Make sure boats and gear are consolidated well before the scheduled departure time.

Accessing for Paddlers from the US

American paddlers usually arrive in the Canadian Gulf Islands via Vancouver and then head over to the Gulf Islands via ferry. The 2 mainland ferry terminals at Tsawwassen and Horseshoe Bay provide the quickest access to Vancouver Island and subsequently to Victoria, Nanaimo and the Gulf Islands. For information and schedules for these and other BC Ferries refer to the previous "Ferries" section.

Two other ferry options provide access to the Canadian Gulf Islands for those arriving from the States. The first is the Washington State Anacortes Ferry which departs from Anacortes and arrives in Sidney (just north of Victoria) twice daily. This ferry provides vehicle service. For more information go to: www.wsdot.wa.gov/ferries/ or call 1-888-808-7977.

The second option is the Coho Ferry. Operated by Blackball Transport this car ferry departs from Port Angeles arriving in downtown Victoria twice daily (3 times daily in peak summer periods). For more information and schedules go to: www.cohoferry.com.

While it is possible to paddle across from the American San Juans, I don't reccommend doing so unless you are a very experienced paddler. The nearest Canada Customs check-ins are either Bedwell Harbour on South Pender Island or Sidney

Launching

Suitable launch sites are found adjacent to most terminals in the Gulf Islands. Some are easier to access than others; none require paying a fee and all are described in detail under the launch sections in this book. Generally, distances between the ferry dock and water accesses are short, with the longest distance experienced by paddlers disembarking from the ferry at Swartz Bay. Boat wheels eliminate some of the inconvenience of this particular 0.5 km (0.3 mi) distance.

Occasionally marinas provide the most convenient launch locations. Most charge a minimal fee (from $5 to $8) for the use of their ramp and associated parking facilities. In my experience, the operators have been most courteous and in some cases have suggested alternative procedures so as to avoid the congestion of vehicles, trailers and boats that surround the ramp. For these extras and for the convenience provided, I gladly pay the minimal fee.

All along the coast of BC there are public wharves, easily recognized by their bright red railings. The floats attached to the wharves are used for moorage by many boaters, yet for paddlers who are willing to lower themselves into their boat from up to 1 m (3 ft) above, they are a convenient launch.

Throughout the islands, and in urban areas on Vancouver Island, there are designated public beach accesses that provide short distance access to shoreline. Many of these are convenient launch locations, and most have nearby parking space.

Navigation Charts

The Canadian Hydrographic Services publishes charts for all of the areas covered in this guidebook. They are 3440 Race Rocks to Darcy; 3441 Haro Strait, Boundary Pass and Satellite Channel; 3442 North Pender to Thetis Island; 3443 Thetis Island to Nanaimo. All these charts are the same scale, 1:40,000. This scale serves kayakers well.

There is a cruising atlas, No. 3313, also published by the Canadian Hydrographic Services. Although it contains interesting supplemental information on weather, distress signals, distance tables and landmarks it's spiral bound, 24–page format is not so convenient for the paddler.

You can check the Canadian Hydrographic Service website at www.charts.gc.ca. Charts are available for purchase at most kayak and marine specialty shops.

H&R Nautical Ventures, has published three sets of strip charts for the Gulf islands called "*Small Craft Nautical Maps: Sooke to Nanaimo and the Gulf islands.*" Most of the charts are the 1:40,000 scale. Many paddlers prefer their smaller format. They are sold through most kayak and marine specialty shops.

Daily Distances

Water distances throughout this book are given in nautical miles (nmi). The length of a nautical mile corresponds to latitudinal minutes and is therefore not subject to metrification. The speed at which we cover distances is expressed in knots, and 1 knot equals 1 nautical mile per hour. Most kayakers cruise around 3 knots, meaning we are capable of paddling up to 3 nautical miles in 1 hour.

However, cruising speed and the speed that we actually travel differ for several reasons. First, distances are often calculated following a direct line, yet with a coastline as convoluted as ours, we simply do not paddle a ruler–straight path. (The distances provided in this guide do not take into consideration every single indentation along each of the coastlines described.) Second, we tend to make plenty of stops to explore and stretch. Finally, paddling speed depends upon how fast the water itself is moving. An opposing current with a speed of as little as 1 knot affects a small boater's progress. Taking all these variables into account, most of us travel around 2 knots and comfortably cover 10 nautical miles over an average day. A little determination and favourable currents could well increase this average. However, given normal paddling conditions, figure on 10 mi as a daily average.

Off Season Paddling

Paddle any of the Gulf Islands routes in the winter season, and you are in for a rare treat. Most marine traffic comes to a standstill. It is much quieter. There are more sea birds, the sea lions have returned and the steel–grey waters can be mirror–still.

The brazen among us enjoy the overnight solitude in having an entire marine park to ourselves. Others escape to one of the many Bed and Breakfasts in the Gulf Islands and plan daytime excursions. Those of us fortunate to be living close to the islands head off for a day's paddle, returning to the comforts of home by evening.

But there are conditions present in winter that must be considered prior to heading out.

- It is much colder. Be prepared for lower temperatures and the greater likelihood of rain. Remember your hands and head; pogies or gloves (that will keep you warm even when wet) are considered essential, along with a sou'wester for the rain and a toque for the cold.
- The weather is far less predictable and much less forgiving than in the summer. Winds are generally stronger and rain can be relentless. Pay particular attention to weather forecasts at this time of year, yet be prepared for rapid shifts in both wind direction and intensity.
- Seas reflect the weather conditions. Be prepared for rougher, more unpredictable seas.
- Daylight hours are shorter. Be aware of the passage of time so as to not get caught unprepared by darkness.
- Take full responsibility for your safety. There is far less marine traffic at this time of year, and so the likelihood of having to deal with an emergency without immediate

assistance is far greater. Have a plan of action worked out well in advance with the entire group for dealing with emergencies.

Kayak Specialty Shops, Rentals and Tour Companies

The sea kayak industry on the Pacific coast is alive and well. Many specialty shops and tour companies operate in and around Vancouver, Victoria, Nanaimo and the Gulf Islands. In fact, at least one company is now based on each of the larger Islands. Most of these owner–operated businesses offer complementary ferry pick–up and drop–off services as well as kayak rentals, convenient for those who wish to walk on to the ferry. Others provide accommodation. Paddling with knowledgeable guides who are trained in first aid, safety and navigation is for many, preferable to self–guided exploration. Be sure of the credibility of the company that interests you. Ask questions regarding guiding certification, length of time it has been in business, previous customer service appraisals, safety considerations, etc.

Some kayak businesses have been around for years, some are new, others come and go. Finding up to date information can be a challenge. The most reliable source I have found is accessed through *Wave Length Magazine*, a kayak specialty magazine published in this area. Their comprehensive website maintains an up to date list of tour companies and retailers. Check it out at www. WaveLengthMagazine.com.

Other sources of information are listed at the back of the book.

Marine Weather

The Summer Dry Belt

As the result of a rain shadow cast by Vancouver Island mountain ranges and the Olympic Mountains in Washington State, the Gulf Islands enjoy a relatively dry climate, especially during the summer months. Total annual rainfall rarely exceeds 80 cm (32 in) with Galiano, reportedly the driest of all the islands, receiving less than 57 cm (23 in). Less than 25 percent of the precipitation falls between April and October, and periods of drought extending over four to six weeks are common each summer.

Temperatures are ideal for paddling between May and September. Mean temperatures on the water are over 10 °C (50 °F) and temperatures in July and August average between 15° and 17 °C (approx. 62 °F). Because of the cooling effect of sea breezes, maximum temperatures on the water seldom exceed 23 °C (73 °F).

Winds

Winds in the Strait of Georgia and Juan de Fuca Strait conform to a fairly regular pattern, whereas in the Gulf Islands, they tend to be unpredictable.

In simple terms, two weather regimes establish themselves over this region. One dominates in the summer and the other during the winter. As the summer regime eases in during the spring, the entire Gulf Islands area is subject to strong winds. These winds decrease in frequency, and by summer they are typically calm to light. Winds come up even during fair weather. Lows and fronts can advance in the form of strong southerlies that bring unsettled, rainy weather.

In the Strait of Georgia, northwesterlies not only affect waters within the strait but spill into some of the channels between the Gulf Islands. (Plumper Sound between Saturna and the Penders is often affected by these winds.) In the Juan de Fuca Strait, winds associated with a Pacific high funnel down the strait (blowing up to 20 knots in the afternoon), affecting the waters in eastern Juan de Fuca as well as the Gulf Islands area.

Sea breezes resulting from the differential heating of the land and the water complicate the picture further. They are produced by the greater heating of the land during the day and blow onshore. Usually peaking by mid afternoon, if they are strong enough, they may cause choppy seas.

In the fall, no single wind pattern can be counted on for long. During the winter months, although winds tend to blow from the southeast, they are much more variable, much stronger and blow more frequently. However, even at that time of year, sunny skies and calm weather are possible.

In general, watch for winds from the south during the summer as they tend to bring wet and unstable weather. Be prepared for brisk onshore breezes during the late afternoon. And listen to the continuous weather broadcasts that provide local weather reports and marine weather forecasts for the entire Gulf Islands area.

Wind conditions described in this book apply to the summer months, unless otherwise specified.

Marine Weather Broadcasts

Environment Canada and the Canadian Coastguard provide continuous marine weather broadcasts for the Gulf Islands and Victoria area. To obtain these weather broadcasts by phone call 604–664–9010 or 604–666–3655 (Vancouver) or call 250–363–6880 or 250–363–6492 (Victoria). To obtain marine weather forecasts for the Pacific region on–line go to the Environment Canada site at www.weatheroffice.ec.gc.ca.

On the water it is best to carry a radio that is capable of receiving transmitted broadcasts. A small VHF will pick up at least one of four stations on frequencies (MHz) WX1, WX2, WX3 and 21B. The smaller, less expensive weather radios will pick up two or three of these same stations.

During the broadcast a general synopsis is provided of systems that will most likely affect coastal waters. In addition, local weather conditions provided by the various reporting stations throughout the Gulf Islands and eastern Juan de Fuca (East Point, Active Pass, Nanaimo, Discovery Point, Trial Islands and Race Rocks) are given. Determine which of these stations is closest to where you plan to paddle. Forecasts are issued four times daily.

An explanation of some of the terms used during these continuous marine weather broadcasts follows.

- Wind speeds are given in knots. (Light means wind speeds of 0–11 knots, moderate is 12–19 knots, strong is 20–33 knots.)
- Both wind and swell directions refer to the direction from which they come.

- Marine wind warnings are issued whenever the winds are expected to rise. The warning frequently heard in this area during the summer is "small craft warning." It is not based on the size of the craft, but on the strength of the wind, and it means 20–33 knot winds are expected.
- The combined wind, wave and swell heights are given in metres.

Remember that no matter what your ability level is, you must always make weather conditions the final deciding factor in your route selection process. Inclement weather drastically changes the suitability of all paddling areas. Make it a habit to listen to marine weather forecasts before heading out on any route.

Although rare in the Gulf Islands, fog can affect paddling conditions. Photo: David Spittlehouse.

Sea Conditions

Tides

The Gulf Islands experience four tides over an approximate twenty–five–hour period a "high" high and a "low" high, a "low" low and a "high" low. The tides fluctuate at their greatest range, 4 m (13 ft), with a new or full moon. These "spring" tides occur approximately twice a month throughout the year. During the moon's first and last quarters the range is generally a little more than half of the "spring" range—referred to as the "neap" tides. (The words "spring" and "neap" are derived from Saxon words meaning "active" and "inactive.")

Tidal predictions for the Gulf Islands appear in *Vol. 5* of the *Tide and Current Tables*, published annually by the Canadian Hydrographic Service. When using the Tide and Current Tables from April through October, add an hour to compensate for Pacific Daylight Time.

The Tide and Current Tables provide water heights for specific places called Reference Ports. Reference Ports for this area include Sooke, Victoria, Fulford Harbour, Vancouver and Point Atkinson. Based on these major references are the Secondary Ports that show corrected times and water heights for local areas. Paddlers who are not familiar with calculating water heights at Secondary Ports can refer to a sample calculations section in the Tide and Current Tables.

Tide predictions are also available on the web. Check the Canadian Hydrographic Services site at www.charts.gc.ca. Follow the links to "Water Levels and Currents."

In the Gulf Islands, tides affect paddlers in one of two ways. First, the tides determine water levels onshore. During the summer the lower low tide generally occurs in the morning and the higher high water occurs at night. This means that kayaks and canoes need to be pulled high enough so that they do not float away in the middle of the night. It also means that boats and gear will be carried a longer distance back to the water than they were carried the evening before. The second way that tides affect paddlers is that they also affect current speeds. The strength of currents is roughly proportionate to the difference between high and low water.

Currents

Flooding and ebbing tides in the Gulf Islands create flows that usually run up to 1 and 2 knots. However, they can reach 10 knots in the narrow passes between some islands. When tidal streams reach these speeds, passage by paddle craft is made difficult not only by the fast–moving water but also by the eddies, and standing waves that are encountered. These hazards present the greatest danger to paddlers; subsequently, narrow passes must be entered during slack water when there is little or no current.

Slack water (or times of minimum flow) can be predicted using the *Tide and Current Tables, Vol. 5*, or the Current Atlas.

The Tide and Current Tables provide maximum flow and slack water times at specific places called Reference Stations. Reference Sta-

A winter paddle in heavy swell off Oak Bay. Photo: Andrew Madding.

tions within the islands include Race Passage, Active Pass, Porlier Pass, Gabriola Passage and Dodd Narrows. Based on these major references are the Secondary Stations that show corrected times and flow speeds for local areas. Paddlers who are not familiar with calculating current speeds at Secondary Stations can refer to a sample calculations section in the Tide and Current Tables.

The Current Atlas is comprised of charts that provide pictorial representation of current flows in the Gulf Islands on an hourly basis. It is easy to use and it gives an overall picture of currents, allowing paddlers to determine the best overall route plan.

For the Gulf Islands, use the Canadian Hydrographic Service's Current Atlas: *Juan de Fuca Strait to Strait of Georgia*. Determine which of the charts to refer to by using the Tide and Current Tables and making some calculations, or purchase either *Washburne's Tables* or *Murray's Tables*, available at most kayak specialty shops. These simple–to–use reference tables are published annually and take you directly to the right chart in the atlas for any hour of any day without any calculations.

Current predictions are also available on the web. Check the Canadian Hydrographic Services site at www.charts.gc.ca. Follow the links to "Water Levels and Currents." Predictions for Reference Stations are provided. Secondary Stations predictions are not found on the site.

Knowing the direction and speed of currents is useful not only for predicting when to avoid certain areas but also because currents can be used to your advantage. Tides in the Gulf Islands tend to flood to the north and ebb to the south. With knowledge of this general pattern, the paddler would benefit by paddling south in the morning (with an ebb tide) and north in the afternoon (with a flood). Consult the Current Atlas while planning your trip as it details the exceptions to this general pattern.

Other Sea Conditions

Sea conditions are not only affected by strong currents. Other less predictable factors can lead to the presence of rip tides and steep standing waves.

Here are a few examples.

- The highest and steepest waves in this area occur when strong currents oppose wind–generated waves. For instance, when northward flooding waters leave Porlier Pass and encounter a northwest wind, steep waves result.
- When the downstream side of an island is surrounded by shallows, tide rips are common.
- When currents converge, turbulent waters result. (A good example of this is off East Point where currents from Tumbo Channel collide with those from Boundary Pass. The seas are made more tumultuous by the adjacent shallows.)
- Off headlands, increased wind, currents and rebounding waves create chaotic seas.

It is well beyond the range of this particular book to detail all conditions that create such difficult waters. Neither are the skills necessary for paddling through hazardous waters outlined in this text. Other books do a far better job of covering both of these topics. Check with a kayak specialty shop to determine which titles they recommend.

Sea Temperatures

Water temperatures in the Gulf Islands fall to about 7°C (44°F) in winter and seldom exceed 13°C (55°F) in the summer. Most paddlers will never experience the threat of such chilling waters, but this is a hazard that must be considered, first by eliminating the likelihood of a capsize and second by knowing what to do in the event of one.

Refer to "Safety Considerations" on the next page.

Fog

Fog is a hazard over the eastern part of Juan de Fuca, forming most frequently in the summer and fall.

Although visibility in the Gulf Islands is rarely affected by fog, it is affected by low–lying cloud and drizzle. Statements regarding visibility are made during marine weather broadcasts if it is expected to be reduced to less than 6 nautical miles.

Safety Considerations

The paddler's first line of defence in dealing with a potentially risky situation is to not get into the situation in the first place. Too often time schedules dictate when we go paddling rather than the conditions out there. Know what to expect by listening to weather forecasts—before you go. Determine where there are potentially hazardous waters, and work out a schedule to avoid paddling through at times of high risk. Select routes appropriate to your paddling abilities.

Accidents still occur, even when paddlers are experienced and prepared. Have a plan worked out on how to deal with any number of emergencies—well in advance of their occurrence. If you do capsize it is critical to get out of the water in as short a time as possible. Practise both solo and group rescue techniques before your trip.

Emergency Safety Equipment

Consider carrying the following emergency safety equipment.

- Consider carrying a VHF (two–way radio) – If for some reason you cannot get out of the water, you must be able to alert others that you need help.
- Flares – Three pyrotechnic distress signals (distress flares) kept within easy reach.
- Personal Flotation Device – The Canadian Coast Guard advises boaters to wear a personal flotation device (PFD) that has enough positive buoyancy to keep the wearer's head well above the water in case they are immersed. Most capsize victims initially experience something referred to as "cold water shock" during which

Riding the current off Trial Island.
Photo: Andrew Madding.

the heart rate increases up to two times its normal rate and breathing increases five times its normal rate. If this person is not wearing a PFD with adequate buoyancy, the effect of their body's reaction to immersion, along with panic and the presence of waves, can lead to their inhaling water and, possibly, to their drowning.

- Pump – to remove water from the cockpit in the event of a capsize.
- Paddle Float – to assist with a rescue
- Watertight Storage Bag – for extra clothing.
- First Aid Kit
- Whistle

Hypothermia
Hypothermia (body heat loss that can cause death) could result with prolonged exposure to cold. Getting out of the water and back onshore are critical in dealing with this condition, but once ashore, obtaining dry clothing and allowing the body core to return to normal temperatures are essential. Paddlers should familiarize themselves with the symptoms and treatment of hypothermia.

Communication in an Emergency
In the event of an emergency good communication will prove critical. Let someone know of your route plan before you go. Inform them as well of your safe arrival to avoid costly and unnecessary searches by search and rescue organizations. In the event that you require emergency assistance any of the following methods will alert others of the need for help.

- VHF Radio – Frequency 156.8 MHhz channel 16. Signal Maday (3 times) indicating your name and position and the type of assistance you require.
- Distress Flares – flares burn for several seconds to a minute and can be seen for several miles.
- Distress Signal – 3 signals at intervals of about one minute – a whistle or a flashlight.
- Cellular – dial *16
- Coast Guard Marine Emergency Number 1-800-567-5111 or 1-800-661-9202

The Canadian Coastguard has published an easy to read guide called the *Sea Kayaking Safety Guide*. It is available at no cost. Check your kayak specialty shop – many of them carry it.

Marine Traffic
Some areas within the Gulf Islands are busier than others with boat traffic. For instance, both motorized and sailing craft tend to converge on the narrow passes between the islands at slack water. Sea–going barges and tugs towing log booms are particularly threatening; wait for both tug and boom to pass through. Busier still are the congested areas around large marinas. The Sidney area is particularly busy with the traffic that enters and exits Tsehum Harbour and Canoe Bay. Most small boaters (sail and power boaters) exhibit a polite awareness of paddlers, but I have heard of encounters that have been unpleasant and, in one instance, quite frightening. If in doubt as to whether your presence has been noticed, attempt some sort of

Waiting for the ferry to pass in Trincomali Channel. Photo: Kelly Irving.

communication with oncoming craft. In most cases, a wave of the hand or paddle is sufficient.

Larger vessels—seiners, huge ships and ferries—demand a paddler's respect simply because of their size and lack of manoeuvrability. Large freighters follow the major shipping routes out in the middle of Juan de Fuca and Boundary Pass, so unless a paddler is crossing these open bodies of water, these vessels are of little concern. Ferries, on the other hand, run frequently between Tsawwassen and Swartz Bay and between the Gulf Islands and pose the greatest threat in a number of ways. First of all, the large ferries run close to 20 knots. That is five times faster than we can paddle! If you must cross their path, determine quickly whether you are on a collision course. To do this, hold a steady course (by referring to your compass or a distant landmark), then note the position of the ferry relative to your bow. If the angle relative to your bow and the ferry increases as you converge, this indicates that you will pass beyond the intersection point. If the angle remains the same, you are on a collision course. If there is any doubt as to whether you can make the crossing safely, wait until the ferry has passed. Remember, a kayak or canoe is far more manoeuvrable than a ferry and can achieve a full stop easily. In these instances, your safety is entirely your responsibility.

Ferries also create swell. On their own these ferry–generated waves are of little concern. It is when they wash onshore or over shallows that trouble could occur. In calm water, an unexpected break could catch the unsuspecting paddler off guard. Onshore, boats left at the water line are swamped by these large ferry waves that dump on the beach.

One final caution—pay particular attention around ferry docks. Watch that ferries are not about to exit or enter the slip, and stay clear of prop wash. In a hurried attempt to meet a return sailing, I cut across the slip dock entrance just as the ferry approached. I was reprimanded by attendants concerned not only with the potential collision but also with an awareness that their wash could easily wrap my fibreglass kayak around a piling.

Land Jurisdictions

Private Property and Crown Foreshore

Most of the shoreline above the high tide line in this area is private property. This is especially so in the Gulf Islands were recreation properties abound. In Canada, all foreshore between high and low water is Crown land and is legally accessible to the public. In theory, this means paddlers can go ashore anywhere except where foreshore leases have been granted for private wharves, log booming and marina or port facilities. Most of us, however, are not comfortable with sitting in front of someone's private residence, let alone setting up camp a few metres from their front yard. Fortunately, throughout the islands there are many public accessible locations far more enticing. Beaches that are away from private residences, marine parks and recreation reserves have greater appeal for overnight stopovers, particularly when tide levels are not excessively high.

BC Marine Parks

Several marine parks, administered by BC Parks, are found throughout the Canadian Gulf Islands. The larger parks, including Montague Harbour and Pirate's Cove have developed facilities largely catering to recreational boaters and, in the case of Montague Harbour, also to drive–in campers. Other parks such as Dionisio on Galaino Island, Wallace Island and Wakes Cove on Valdes Island are smaller and developed on a limited basis.

Due to increased use, BC Parks is understandably implementing changes to further protect resources. These changes include the creation of designated campsites, the installation of sanitary facilities and the enforcement of a "No Fires" policy. This includes below–the–high–tide–line beach fires.

There are no garbage disposal facilities within marine parks, except at Montague Harbour. Whatever you pack in, you pack out. Camping fees? Yes, but very reasonable rates apply. Check the BC Parks website for an up–to–date list of the fees applied for each marine park. The website provides additional information on the Marine Parks located within this region. Check it out at www.bcparks.ca.

The Gulf Islands National Park Reserve

In 1995 the Canadian and BC governments established a program to promote the protection of marine environments on the Pacific coast with the hope of the eventual formation of a new national park within the Canadian Gulf Islands. The park would be established, over time, with the transfer of provincial and provincial marine parks, ecological reserves and unoccupied crown lands and islets to Canada. These transferred lands would make up approximately one half of the park with the other half being comprised of lands purchased under the Pacific Marine Heritage Legacy program.

The long–awaited, Gulf Islands National Park Reserve, was announced in 2003 with the official transfer of 9 provincial and marine parks, 2 ecological reserves and various crown lands and islets. Acquired properties including James Bay on Prevost Island, Russell and Tumbo Islands, Taylor Point and Narvaez Bay on Saturna Island. Georgeson Island and Bennett Bay on Mayne Island were also transferred. Twenty–nine separate properties on 16 islands now make up the park's 5,900 hectares or 59 km². Given the separation between the parklands the operational area of the park covers approximately 725 km² roughly defined by D'Arcy Island to the south, Cabbage and Tumbo islands to the east, Prevost Islands' James Bay to the north and Portland and Sidney Islands to the west.

Given the extensive recreational usage and development in the Gulf Islands region this national park contains the highest number of designated species at risk of any park in the Parks Canada system. Ecological integrity is the primary goal of the national park and will be the primary consideration in management planning. Levels of access and land usage will be determined over a period of several years and will vary based largely on the protection of this unique coastal environment.

Parks Canada will continue to allow recreational usage for the next several years in areas previously offering this experience to paddlers. Undesignated camping on former provincial Crown lands will be reviewed. This will help park managers determine if the impact of camping on some of the more fragile areas will require camping restrictions, or the development of designated campsites. Kayakers are encouraged to participate in the public consultation process to make their views known, and to share their knowledge about kayaking routes with park managers.

For more information on the new national park reserve, contact Parks Canada at (250) 654–4000 or check their website at www.gulfislands.pc .gc.ca.

Ecological Reserves

There are presently 120 ecological reserves in BC, preserved because of the unique flora, fauna or marine life represented. They are largely established on Crown land, although in some cases private property has been purchased by non–profit organizations and leased back to the Ecological Reserves Program.

Seven ecological reserves (Canoe Islets, Rose Islets, Race Rocks, Oak Bay Islands, Brackman Island, Trial Islands and Ten Mile Point) are easily accessed by shallow–draft boats in the Gulf Islands area. Whereas casual non–consumptive, non–motorized use is permitted on most reserves in the province, these areas are particularly delicate (many protect nesting sea birds). They are not intended for public recreational use, and although not strictly prohibited, landing is discouraged.

Check out the Friends of Ecological Reserves website for a listing and description of the Ecological Reserves in this area at www.ecoreserves.bc.ca.

A high-tide landing, Thieves Bay, Pender. Photo: Andrew Madding.

First Nation Lands – Indian Reserves

Many of the reserves in the Gulf Islands are uninhabited, and most of them present features that are attractive to paddlers—easy access, wind sheltered shore, and level areas for setting up camp. Often we are tempted to go ashore and stay awhile. However, all reserve property is private—owned by the various First Nation bands living on Vancouver Island.

In researching for the book, I asked each First Nation band what their policy was with regard to paddlers landing on reserves. Their individual requests follow.

Valdes Island Reserve Lands

The three reserves on Valdes are owned and administered by the Lyackson First Nation Band in Ladysmith. Paddlers wanting to visit any of the reserves on Valdes must obtain written permission from the Band Chief. You can contact the Chief through the Lyackson Band office by calling 250– 246–5019 or by writing to the Band Chief, Lyackson Band Office, 9137 Chemainus Road, Ladysmith, B.C., V0R 1K5.

Tent Island

The Penelakut First Nation Band (on Kuper Island) do permit camping on Tent Island. The Penelakut ask that you contact them by phone at which time they will grant permission to land on Tent Island. They will also request a donation. (The Penelakut forwards donations to a worthy community cause. For example in 2004 donations went to the Childrens Fund.) You can reach the Penelakut Band by calling 250–246–2321.

Fiddlers Cove, Saturna Island

Fiddlers Cove adjacent to Narvaez Bay on Saturna Island is under the jurisdiction of the Tsawout First Nation Band. The Tsawout Band is based in Saanichton, north of Victoria. Tsawout requests that you call or provide a written request prior to landing or camping at Fiddler's Cove. Requests to camp are most often granted with a letter of confirmation from the Tsawout. The band will ask for a donation to their Elders Group. Phone the band office at 250–652–9101 and ask to speak to the Lands Administrator or address enquiries to Lands Administrator, Tsawout Band, Box 121, Saanichton, BC, V8M 2C3.

Chatham and Discovery Islands

Chatham and Discovery reserves are under the jurisdiction of the Victoria–based Songhees First Nation Band. At one time the Songhees permitted daytime visitors. However, two fires in the 1990s led to the public closure of reserve lands on both Chatham and Discovery. The band monitors the area and will ask those found trespassing to leave. In 2004 there was no indication that this policy would change. For updated information, call the Songhees Band office in Victoria at 250–386–1043 or address enquiries to 1500A Admirals Road, Victoria, BC, V9A 2R1.

Becher Bay

The Becher Bay Band asks that paddlers contact the band office prior to landing on any of the reserve lands around Becher Bay. The band permits day time stops on their land but no overnight camping. They request no fires. Make enquiries by calling the band office at 250–478–3535 or writing to the Becher Bay Band, 3843 East Sooke Road, Box #4, RR #1, Sooke, BC, V0S 1N0.

Department of National Defence (DND) Lands

Whether or not Crown foreshore is accessible to the public on DND lands appears to depend on how the federally owned land is being used. In an emergency, landing on the beaches fronting DND property is legitimate; however, when military reserves such as those around Rocky Point are used as a munitions depot, security tightens, and small boaters are discouraged from landing anywhere in the vicinity for their own safety. The firing ranges at Albert Head are intermittently used for training. Once again, for their own safety, boaters are discouraged from landing. There are no DND lands at all in the Gulf Islands. The few that are within the area covered by this book are located in the Sooke/Metchosin area.

Camping

Where To Camp

This guide book highlights the many camping location scattered throughout this area. Most campsites are those designated as such by both BC Parks and the Gulf Islands National Park Reserve. There are a couple of camping locations identified that are on Crown Land.

I've heard paddlers express concern that their need for solitude will not be met by park–designated sites. In some ways their concern is valid, especially on summer weekends and around parks that also cater to the needs of the yachting crowd. Yet by selecting camping areas without mooring buoys, wharves and protected anchorages, particularly in the lesser–developed marine parks, paddlers can avoid crowded locations. With shallow–draft boats they can also access areas that pleasure boats cannot. For instance, at Pirate's Cove Marine Park, a very popular moorage site is avoided by heading to an adjacent bay that is too exposed for sailors. Head to camping locations that are unpopular with the cruising set. Chances are that your group will be the only company you keep.

Water

Always carry your own water supply rather than depend on water in an area where summer rains are so infrequent that ground water deficits often occur. Although several marine parks have pumps they can not always be relied upon.

Three litres (approx. 3 qt) per person per day will suffice with some

Secluded campsite near Saltspring Island. Photo: Andrew Madding.

to spare if you are held over by bad weather. Sea water is fine for washing dishes, especially if followed by a fresh–water rinse.

Fires

There are wilderness regions on the Pacific coast where fire danger is minimal, but in an area that receives a mere 75 cm (30 in) of rain a year and experiences weeks of summertime drought, fire is a number one threat. During drought periods, July through September, the BC Forest Service prohibits all fires in this area. Assume during any summertime trip that this ban is in effect. This ban includes building fires on beaches below the high tide mark. Bring a small backpacking stove for cooking.

Shellfish Harvesting and Fishing

Very few paddlers are tempted to collect shellfish during the summer due to the threat of paralytic shellfish poisoning (PSP). For those unfamiliar with PSP, this is a hazard of which you should be aware.

Clams, oysters and mussels can contain a poison that is harmful to humans. These shellfish are filter feeders,which means that they strain the sea water through their gills, extracting the minute organisms for food. From the spring through the fall, a tiny diatom, Gonyaulax, appears in concentrations much larger than normal. It collects in the muscle tissue of various filter feeders, and although it does not harm the bivalve, if the toxins are taken in sufficient quantities, they can make humans very sick and in rare cases can be fatal.

It is impossible for the average person to distinguish between poisonous and safe molluscs. In Canada the federal fisheries department monitors the threat of PSP. Since it is impossible to routinely check every bay and inlet, a general ban is imposed on the collection of shellfish from May through October in many areas surrounding Vancouver Island, including the Gulf Islands and Barkley Sound.

Rather than collect shellfish, try your luck at fishing. Although the best sport fishing occurs in the winter, springs and cohos can be caught along with small chinook and bottomfish. In Canada finfish fishing requires a license, available from most tackle shops and marinas. For information about sport fishing licenses, Canadian fishing regulations and species limits have a look at the Department of Fisheries and Oceans website www.pac.dfo-mpo.gc.ca.

Animals – Safety Considerations

There are regions on the Pacific coast where animals present a safety risk to visitors. Such is not the case in the Gulf Islands. Coastal species that pose a potential threat such as the wolf and bear left this region long ago. The rare cougar sighting in the Sooke/Metchosin area does not constitute cause for concern to paddlers visiting that area.

Racoons and crows will take food left out in the open. Securing food in a sealed kayak hatch will take care of this concern.

Protecting our Marine Environment

Did you know that less than one percent of BC's coastal waters have protected status?

Although a large conservation area has been established with the formation of the Gulf Islands National Park Reserve so far the park has a largely terrestrial focus. In 1998 two Marine Protected Area pilot projects in the Southern Gulf islands area – Race Rocks and Gabriola Passage were announced by the federal government. In 2003 they remain as pilot projects and are unlikely to win official designation anytime soon. Also in 2003 Parks Canada made a commitment to establish a National Marine Conservation Area that would give protected status to marine environments, including possible no-fishing zones, throughout the southern Gulf Islands.

With these initiatives government has demonstrated movement in the direction of protection. However progress is slow and is not likely to speed up with competing interests, considerations related to aboriginal treaty negotiations and other challenges.

Some believe that citizen-led efforts hold the best hope in winning protection for marine habitats. The Georgia Strait Alliance (GSA) has been committed to marine protection in this area since the early 90s. It has worked on a number of fronts to raise public awareness, inform decision-makers and develop solutions to the many pressures that threaten marine habitats. (GSA Website)

The GSA has joined forces with other grassroot organizations on both sides of the border to form a cross-border marine protected area – the Orca Pass International Stewardship Area. Orca Pass hopes to win protected status for environmental hotspots within the Georgia Strait/Puget Sound marine ecosystem. Their vision is perhaps best summed up in this comment. "Most likely the Orca Pass Stewardship Area will be established in stages over several years, through a patchwork of regulatory and voluntary mechanisms on both sides of the border….a stitching together of measures that will eventually form a large cohesive quilt of marine conservation." (Laurie MacBride, GSA's Executive Director)

It takes massive effort to work toward the protection of our marine environment. Water borne travelers, such as we are, experience the natural beauty of our ocean waters frequently. Perhaps then we have an added responsibility to do what we can to protect them. Consider playing some part, however small. Volunteer for a local conservation agency. Make a donation to the Georgia Strait Alliance or Orca Pass. And keep yourself informed. Here are some websites to get you started:

Parks Canada
www.gulfislands.pc.gc.ca
Georgia Strait Alliance
www.georgiastrait.org
Orca Pass
www.pugetsound.org/orcapass
Gulf Islands Trust
www.islandtrust.bc.ca
Friends of Ecological Reserves
www.ecoreserves.bc.ca

Paddling Etiquette

Paddlers and the Environment

Few paddlers intentionally disrupt wildlife, but we do affect them none-theless—simply because we get in close to their natural habitat.

Harbour seals and sea lions are often encountered. Most vulnerable are harbour seals with their young, especially when paddlers, alarmed to find what appears to be an abandoned pup, try to rescue the orphan. More than likely the mother and pup have been separated for a short period of time while the mother has gone off in search of food. Wait before assuming the pup cannot possibly make it without your assistance.

Dozens of powered craft can pass by a group of seals hauled out on the rocks, and these magnificent mammals barely lift a flipper. Yet as soon as we pass by, they scurry into the water as fast as they are able. Rather than encourage this frantic scramble, if you see a haul–out spot covered with seals, swing well out and you will be able to more easily observe the seals. Paddlers with binoculars have a distinct advantage here.

Sea lions are seemingly not intimi-dated by us; in fact, in most cases it is quite the opposite. Paddlers at-tempting to get too close have raised the ire of these large beasts, who then take to the water, swimming to and fro and commanding the intruder's respect simply because of their enor-mous size. Keep a respectable dis-tance away from sea lions, and they will likely remain stationary on the low–tide rocks. Check the Fisheries

Binoculars allow this paddler to observe a nesting site from a respectable distance. Photo: Bruce Holland.

and Oceans Marine Mammal viewing guidelines at http://www-comm.pac.dfo-mpo.gc.ca/pages/MarineMammals/view_e.htm.

Birds are particularly sensitive to our presence during the nesting season. The success or failure of a breeding season could depend on our respect for nesting territory. Avoid paddling close to nesting sites from May through August. Do not land on any of the island colonies at this time of year.

I presume that the term "minimum impact" is familiar to most. Rather than elaborate on "how–to," I will reinforce the merits of "leave no trace camping" in this particular area.

Throughout the Pacific Northwest, paddle sports are increasing in popularity, particularly sea–kayaking. With our new sea–borne mobility and our desire for solitude, we are using areas that had few visitors in the past. As individuals or as a single group we have little effect on our environment, but as our numbers increase, we begin to exert a fair influence. Marine environments require special care so that our collective impact is minimal.

Paddlers and Residents Onshore

I felt it was necessary to include this section to emphasize the importance of a positive relationship between Gulf Islands' residents and paddlers. It is onshore that we encounter the locals, and this is where we need to exercise the most consideration.

Show respect for the privacy of shoreline residents by staying below the high tide line and, prior to exploring inland, requesting their permission to do so. Their largest concerns centre around fire and litter. By introducing ourselves, explaining our intent and putting them at ease by displaying a common–sense respect for the area, we ensure that future paddlers will be welcome visitors.

When possible, buy locally. Often paddlers are so completely self–sufficient that little is required from local proprietors. We simply pay the launch fee (most often the launch is free), and we are off. Consider buying last–minute provisions at local shops, and en route, restock by purchasing from stores associated with marina complexes. Many of these small facilities depend almost entirely on summertime patronage.

Paddlers and the Cultural Environment

Paddlers that visit this area are bound to come across evidence of the native culture that once flourished in this entire area. Shell middens are the most obvious of the features remaining. Cultural features such as these must be respected. They have been here in some instances for thousands of years and an assurance that they remain depends on how we treat them today. Do not tamper with them in any way and do not remove anything from these historically significant areas. Picking away at a shell midden only compounds the erosion that already whittles away at these shell deposits.

The importance of preserving all cultural features by leaving all archaeological sites as they were cannot be overemphasized. Take a look at these features but do not disturb them.

1 Sooke, Metchosin

Paddlers who want to experience the spectacular surf–swept landscape typically associated with the exposed west coast will want to explore this area. Within an hour from Victoria you can paddle jagged shorelines where the ocean spray and sounds of the surge leave a lasting sensory impression. Don't miss Race Rocks. Exposed to extreme tidal action this area presents marine life that is rich in diversity and abundance. Those of you preferring an easier route will not be disappointed. You can retreat to the quiet shallows of Witty's Lagoon where over 160 bird species have been identified. No matter which trip you select, views across Juan de Fuca Strait to the snow–capped peaks of the Olympic Mountains will enhance your time here.

Beacher Bay from Cheanuh Marina. Photo: Mary Ann Snowden.

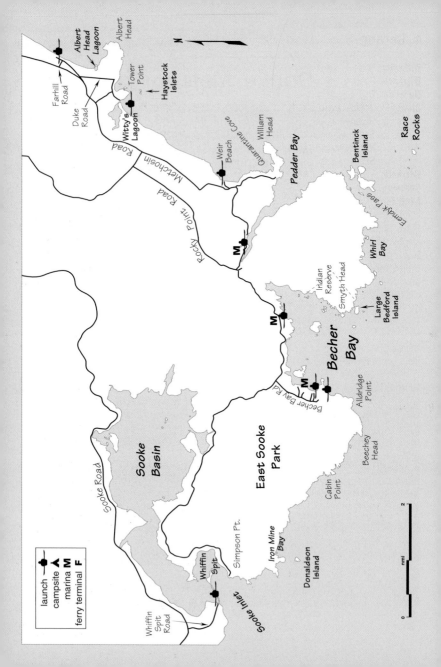

1 Becher Bay To Whiffin Spit

Difficulty Intermediate conditions – moderate risk
Distance 6 nmi one way
Duration Day trip
Charts 3440, Race Rocks to D'Arcy Island (1:40,000)
Tides Reference Port: Sooke
    Secondary Ports: Sooke Basin and Becher Bay
    Reference Port: Victoria
    Secondary Port: William Head
Currents Reference Station: Race Passage
Camping No camping
Land Jurisdictions Capital Regional District (CRD) Parks – East Sooke Park

Here is an incredible opportunity to experience an exposed coast without having to travel to the distant west coast. Explore windswept bluffs and craggy foreshore and get in for a close–up look at a unique spectrum of marine life especially adapted to survive rigorous sea conditions. View the only petroglyph in BC to receive heritage status, visible from the water near Alldridge Point.

Paddling Considerations

During the summer, the prevailing westerlies that blow down Juan de Fuca Strait often build strength during the day and reach maximum speeds by late afternoon. Winds are generally much stronger here than in the Gulf Islands, so listen to wind predictions prior to paddling, paying particular attention to conditions reported from the station at Race Rocks.

Even in calm weather, Pacific swell rolls down the strait. These rollers pose little threat on their own; it is when they break onshore or over shallows that they become threatening. Be on a continuous lookout for offshore breakers.

Fog banks that roll down from the open Pacific can affect visibility in this area, especially in the late summer and early fall. Listen to fog predictions for Juan de Fuca Strait prior to paddling, and always carry a compass.

Because winds are common, and because landings along this exposed stretch of coast are infrequent, this route is recommended for experienced paddlers only.

Getting There and Launching

This trip is accessed using launches in the Sooke/Metchosin area, west of Victoria. The route can be paddled from east to west by launching from Becher Bay or from east to west by using the Whiffin Spit launch.

The Becher Bay launches are accessed from Victoria by following the Old Island Highway (Highway 1A) and then Sooke Road (Highway 14). Turn left at the Metchosin turn–off onto Metchosin Road. Follow Metchosin Road to Happy Valley Road. Turn right, and within 0.5 km (0.3 mi), turn left onto Rocky Point Road. Follow it to

Whiffin Spit looking across to east Sooke Park.
Photo: Mary Ann Snowden.

the junction at East Sooke Road. Continue along East Sooke Road, looking to the left for the Cheanuh Marina, the first of three launches on Becher Bay. The Cheanuh Marina is owned and operated by the Becher Bay Indian Band. They charge a minimal fee for a kayak launch. Plenty of parking space is available.

The second Becher Bay launch is accessed by continuing along East Sooke Road to Becher Bay Road. Turn left and follow Becher Bay Road to Pacific Lions Marina. The operators charge a minimal fee to launch and park vehicles. The marina is closed from October to April.

The final Becher Bay launch is accessed by continuing along Becher Bay Road to East Sooke Park. There is a parking lot at the entrance to the park and a hike of approximately 300 m (1000 ft) to get to the beach launch. The well–marked trail cuts through the old Aylard Farm and ter-

minates at a stairway that leads down to a sandy beach launch.

The Whiffin Spit launch is accessed from Victoria by following the Old Island Highway (Highway 1A) to Sooke Road (Highway 14). Follow Sooke Road to just past the centre of Sooke, turn left onto Whiffin Spit Road. To reach the launch from the large parking area at the end of Whiffin Spit Road carry kayaks over the drift logs on the south–facing shore.

It takes about an hour to get to the launches from Victoria.

Assuming the route is paddled one way a car shuttle is required.

The Route

The route is described here from east to west – Becher Bay to Whiffin Spit. It can, however, be paddled from west to east.

Juan de Fuca Petroglyphs

There are seven known petroglyphs along Juan de Fuca Strait, all made using a process called bruising. The hardness of the rock in Juan de Fuca required the bruising technique and resulted in impressions that are hard to see. On the other hand, the Gulf Islands petroglyphs were carved into the softer sandstones, leaving a much deeper impression.

The two Juan de Fuca petroglyphs that are the easiest to see, especially for paddlers as they can be viewed from the water, are at Alldridge Point. The others on Large Bedford, Beechey Head Islet and Otter Point are much more difficult to locate.

When were these petroglyphs made? This is a difficult question to answer for several reasons. First, petroglyphs contain no organic matter and so cannot be radiocarbon dated. Second, there is often no cultural deposit such as a midden site associated with petroglyphs which could

be used to estimate when they were created. Finally, the design of the Alldridge Point petroglyphs, although simple, does not necessarily prove that they are older or more primitive than others. The stone in which the figures were executed was such a difficult medium that this alone could explain the simplistic forms.

The second Alldridge Point petroglyph appears to represent a fish and, although fainter, is visible on a rockface west of the sea monster. Because some petroglyphs were used to indicate a particularly good fishing ground, perhaps this one marks the exceptional fishing grounds off the point.

In 1927 the Alldridge Point petroglyphs became an official Provincial Heritage Site. It is one of the few designated sites of native origin, and under heritage laws it is protected against any type of defacement.

A major part of this route follows East Sooke Park, a large area covering 1,400 ha (3,500 ac), stretching from Aylard Farm around Beechey Head to Iron Mine Bay and north to Anderson Cove. There are over 60 km (37 mi) of trails in the park with one trail running parallel to the coast. Paddlers using the park launch will hike through an old orchard that was part of the early 1900s' operations at Aylard Farm.

From the Becher Bay launch sites, head toward Alldridge Point and two petroglyphs "bruised" into a rock face on the inside of the exposed drying reefs located off the point. The "sea monster" is the best known of the Juan de Fuca petroglyphs and is easily seen from the water.

Currents are strong around Beechey Head, with eddylines and whorls common during maximum floods and ebbs. Paddle the backeddies close to shore to avoid major turbulence, and exercise caution when wind–generated waves are made steeper upon meeting an opposing ebb tide.

If conditions permit, paddle the windswept coast between Beechey Head and Simpson Point closely, as these shores support a unique spectrum of marine life. Look for blood stars, flower–shaped anemones, purple sea stars, black chitons and the clusters of gooseneck barnacles and California mussels that are most often associated with exposed headlands.

An exceptional cove northwest of Beechey Head is one of the few that provide a protected beach landing. The area is known locally as Cabin Point, although it is not labelled as such on the chart. An unnamed islet best marks the locale of this stopover. Access the beach by paddling along the east side of it. A fish–shaped petroglyph is located on the islet facing to the southeast. I was fortunate to have someone show it to me. If discouraged by what might otherwise be a difficult search, hike across the headland to the shelter on Cabin Point. This is the "Trap Shack," home to the men who once operated fish traps off Beechey Head. In the early part of this century, pile–driven weir traps were placed along the annual migration route of the salmon, providing the most efficient means of catching the fish to date. The fish trap found along these shores operated into the 1950s.

Iron Mine Bay north of Donaldson Island also has a gravel beach suitable for landing. The horseshoe–shaped cove is sheltered from prevailing westerlies, and tide–pooling is splendid on the rocky promontories surrounding the beach. In an emergency paddlers could pull out here and hike 20 minutes up the obvious trail to a parking lot at the end of East Sooke Road.

The 1 nmi–long crossing from Simpson Point to Whiffin Spit is exposed to winds and heavy seas. Watch for turbulence if winds oppose ebb tides flowing out of Sooke Harbour.

Whiffin Spit extends about 1 km (0.6 mi) into Sooke Inlet. The elongated gravel bar forms a natural barrier that protects Sooke Harbour and serves well as a put–in or take–out area for kayakers paddling this route.

2 Weir Beach to Becher Bay

Difficulty Intermediate conditions – moderate risk
Distance 7 nmi one way
Duration Day trip
Charts 3440, Race Rocks to D'Arcy Island (1:40,000)
Tides Reference Port: Sooke, Victoria and William Head
Secondary Ports: Becher Bay
Currents Reference Station: Race Passage
Camping No camping
Land Jurisdictions Indian Reserve – Becher Bay, Department of National Defense – surrounding Pedder Bay and around headland to Church Point.

Fascinating history and spectacular scenery are found all along this route. For several decades a quarantine station stood on these shores, and isolated Bentinck Island was home to a handful of Chinese immigrant lepers, confined to live their final years on a deserted isle. Eemdyk Pass is intriguing, choked with tiny islets, rock reefs and sandy shoals—all supporting an impressive array of marine life. There's some challenging petroglyph exploration to do on Bedford Island, and the alluring beaches nestled in between rock bluffs on Becher Bay are hard to resist.

Paddling Considerations

The stretch from Rocky Point to Becher Bay is exposed to prevailing westerlies. Because these winds come up in the afternoon, consider an early morning start to avoid paddling against them. Listen to wind predictions for Juan de Fuca Strait prior to launching, paying particular attention to reports from the station at Race Rocks.

Strong currents in Race Passage affect the tidal flows in the entire area,

especially in Eemdyk Pass. Avoid the worst of the currents by hugging the shoreline along Rocky Point, or take advantage of tidal streams and schedule paddling so that your direction and flows are the same.

Fog does occur here, especially in the late summer and early fall.

Given the fair likelihood of winds blowing in this area, and that scheduling to avoid stronger currents is required, this route is not recommended for inexperienced paddlers.

Getting There and Launching

This trip is accessed using launches in the Sooke/Metchosin area, west of Victoria. The route can be paddled from east to west by launching at Weir Beach or from west to east by launching at Becher Bay.

To get to the Weir Beach launch from Victoria, follow the Old Island Highway (Highway 1A) and then Sooke Road (Highway 14). Turn left at the Metchosin turn-off onto Metchosin Road. Continue along Metchosin Road by following signs for William Head. Turn left at Sandgate Road. Weir Beach, a public beach access, is found at the terminus of Sandgate, and parking is available nearby. Allow approximately 45 minutes to get to this launch from Victoria.

To get to the Becher Bay launch refer to the launches described in trip 1, Becher Bay to Whiffin Spit.

Assuming this route is paddled one way a car shuttle is required.

The Route

The route is described here from east to west—Weir Beach to Becher Bay. It could as easily be paddled from west to east.

Paddle south from Weir Beach toward Quarantine Cove—so named because from 1894 to 1958 a quarantine station stood on this bay, inspecting all foreign ships bound for Canadian ports. Internment and fumigation buildings housed immigrants suspected of carrying disease. During World War I, eighty thousand Chinese passed through the station. Operations peaked in 1927 when over a thousand ships were inspected (Wolferstan). Remnants of the station wharves are all that remain today.

Paddlers are requested to remain outside the several white and orange buoys surrounding the medium security prison at William Head. One of the prison guards is an avid paddler. Be assured, therefore, that your presence will be noted.

All shoreline from the head of Pedder Bay to just east of Large Bedford Island belongs to the Rocky Point Military Reserve. The area is used for both munitions storage and testing, and although much controversy surrounded its establishment in the 1950s, farms were expropriated and

the reserve was established. Military presence has certainly protected this huge area from development, but landing anywhere along this beautiful stretch of coast is very much discouraged. Public safety is the main concern. Kayakers lured ashore by an inviting cove can expect to be reprimanded if inadvertently discovered by an officer.

Eemdyk Pass, also referred to as "Choked Passage" because of the countless shoals and islets found throughout, is a kayaker's haven. Here, dozens of harbour seals haul out on drying reefs. At low tide, black oystercatchers probe rocky outcrops, and raccoons explore the kelp–covered shores. Otter and mink fish in the shallows.

It is best to paddle the pass close to slack or when tidal flows and route directions are the same. When paddling against the current, take advantage of back eddies and the slower–moving water that is found close to shore. Westerly winds that funnel through this pass could affect paddling progress.

Bentinck Island, once known as the "Island of the Living Dead," has an interesting history. In 1924 the leper colony on D'Arcy Island closed down, and so Bentinck Island, determined at the time to be isolated enough to receive immigrants infected with the disease, became the new station. With the introduction of sulpha drugs, leprosy became curable, and in 1956 the last quarantined leper died on this island. At that time you could apparently rent Bentinck Island at $40 a month. There were no takers. In 1958 the area

Black Oystercatchers

These black, crow–sized birds are easily identified by their long scarlet bill, bright yellow eyes and pink legs. Paddlers are most likely to find them along exposed rock outcrops where they camouflage so well against the dark rocks that we often pass by, unaware of their presence until their shrill incessant call gives them away.

The oystercatcher frequents the rocky surf zone, because it is here that clinging shellfish are so plentiful. The bird's name is a bit of a mis–nomer as it rarely, if ever, eats oysters. They prefer to chip limpets and barnacles off the rocks, but by far this bird's favourite food is mussels.

Banquet time is during the ebb tide, because at this point in the tidal cycle, the shells of the mussel open as the animal sifts the receding waters for plankton. Into the partially opened shell goes the long red bill of the oystercatcher, and with a definitive snip the abductor muscle, which holds the mussel shells together, is cut before it shuts. After working the half–shells apart, the oystercatcher gulps the meat inside. I watched one pair in a tidal flat locate and consume clams at a rate of about one every two minutes.

The oystercatcher lays 2-3 eggs in shallow depressions in bare rock lined with stone and shell chips. The oystercatcher is particularly sensitive during nesting season, May to July. If approached by humans the nesting oystercatcher temporarily abandons their

Black Oystercatcher. Photo Bob Davidson.
Oystercatcher Eggs. Photo: Sherry Kirkvold.

nest leaving it open to predation from less timid birds such as gulls and crows. The success or failure of a breeding season can be determined by our respect for their nesting territory.

was turned over to the Department of National Defence. (Wolferstan).

Although the coves that indent Bentinck look inviting, there are also large numbers of warning signs here that read "Blasting—Keep Out." Arms testing does take place in the area, so it is best to observe this shoreline from your "demilitarized craft."

The notable structure out on Christopher Point is an experimental wind generator. Once it spins, an almost deafening hum is emitted (although paddlers are unlikely to hear it as winds that set the generator in motion are strong). This modern–day windmill marks the north entrance to Whirl Bay, an exposed stretch of shoreline that is steep and rocky. The cove behind Shelter Islet provides the only emergency landing, and the surf zone out on Church Point supports large numbers of gooseneck barnacles and California mussels. From here to Large Bedford, long narrow channels pierce the rock cliffs. Tiny shell beaches provide the only break from the craggy bluffs.

Land on the tombolo that links Large Bedford Island to the main shoreline. (Bedford Island and areas adjacent are on reserve land, and although the natives don't mind paddlers landing on beaches, permission must be obtained from the Becher Bay Band beforehand. (Refer to the Introduction for details.) Climb to the top of Bedford Island for views over Juan de Fuca Strait and across to the Olympics. In the spring, the entire island is covered with white lilies, pink sea–blush and yellow monkey–flowers.

Two petroglyphs representing human faces are apparently located on a sheer rock face on Large Bedford Island. The carvings supposedly face the southeast and cannot be seen from the sea. I have been unsuccessful in my own search for these carved figures, nor have friends, bribed with the promise of reward, come up with their location.

The area surrounding Smyth Head boasts several small coves, white–shell beaches and tiny islets. One particularly inviting cove that faces north offers shelter from the prevailing winds.

Becher Bay was the scene of an incredible massacre in the early 1800s. Only three of three hundred natives survived a raid by invading Nitinat and Clallam Bands. The survivors, a mother, her son and a niece, sought revenge, and so the three waited until most of the attackers had returned to their homelands and only a small guard party remained on Whiffin Spit. Having walked through the night from Becher Bay to Sooke Basin, the mother approached the guarded spit from landward. Meanwhile, her son crossed the water on a raft and approached from the opposite end of the spit. The story goes that they slaughtered the sleeping Clallams and that never again did they enter the Becher Bay territory.

Today the Becher Bay people living at the head of the bay own and operate the Cheanuh Marina. Traditionally, Cheanuh means "salmon"—appropriate today as the marina caters to sport fishermen.

Race Rocks with the Olympic Peninsula in the background. Photo: Andrew Madding.

3 Race Rocks

Difficulty Intermediate conditions – moderate risk
Distance 8 nmi round trip
Duration Day trip
Chart 3440, Race Rocks to D'Arcy Island (1:40,000)
Tides Reference Port: Victoria
Secondary Ports: Pedder Bay and William Head
Currents Reference Station: Race Passage
Camping No camping
Land Jurisdictions Department of National Defence – surrounding Pedder Bay
Ecological Reserve – Race Rocks

Race Rocks offers a marine life presence unrivalled anywhere within the waters surrounding southern Vancouver Island. Strong currents bring a continuous rich supply of plankton to the tiny islets, subsequently drawing large numbers of marine animals. Most impressive are the California and Steller sea lions, especially when viewed from a paddler's vantage. Harbour seals also make the islands their home year round, along with hundreds of pelagic birds. Paddlers may be fortunate to view a pod of orca.

Paddling Considerations

Race Passage is best paddled at slack water; otherwise expect very strong currents, eddies and turbulent water. Because tidal streams reach up to 9 knots in the immediate vicinity of the rocks and up to 6 knots in Race Passage, paddling here demands scheduling. Slack water is brief—currents pick up speed soon after the turn.

The entire area is exposed to prevailing westerlies; therefore it is advisable to listen to marine weather forecasts, paying particular attention to wind predictions for Juan de Fuca Strait. Fog can also occur.

Given these hazardous conditions, Race Rocks is not recommended for the inexperienced. Only those skilled in paddling through fast–moving water and turbulent seas should attempt this route.

Getting There and Launching

Launch from either Weir Beach (refer to trip 2, Weir Beach to Becher Bay) or Pedder Bay Marina.

The Pedder Bay Marina launch is accessed from Victoria by following the Old Island Highway (Highway 1A) and then Sooke Road (Highway 14). Turn left at the Metchosin turn-off onto Metchosin Road. Follow Metchosin Road to Happy Valley Road. Turn right, and within 0.5 km (0.3 mi), turn left onto Rocky Point Road. Follow it to the junction at East Sooke Road. An immediate left here will provide access to the Pedder Bay Marina. The marina charges a minimal fee to launch.

Allow forty–five minutes to drive from Victoria to these launches.

The Route

Launch from the Pedder Bay Marina and pass the beautifully situated Lester Pearson College. The college's doors were opened to international baccalaureate students in 1974. The students and faculty here have played a vital role in ensuring the protection of the unique marine environment at Race Rocks. Today the College acts as the "reserve warden" and provides education opportunities on Great Race as part of the Great Race Marine Research and Education Centre.

The entire coastline along Rocky Point is part of a military reserve, and landings are discouraged. Currents are minimal until just south of Rocky Point, when increased flows start to affect paddling. The farther south and the closer to Race Passage, the stronger the currents and the greater their effect.

If accurate slack–water scheduling and skill permit a safe paddle to Race Rocks, don't miss this exceptional area. The combination of shallows, drying reefs and continuous current creates a highly productive area for marine life. Most obvious are the California and Steller sea lions either basking on the rocks or bobbing in the current. Hundreds of them return to Race Rocks from distant breeding grounds each winter. Nesting sea birds include pelagic cormorants, glaucous–winged gulls, pigeon guillemots and black oyster-catchers. Hundreds of sea birds call this rocky group of islands home each summer. River otters have also taken up residence here, but most spectacular are the pods of orca that occasionally pass through the area. Less obvious, but equally abundant, are mussels, anemones, sponges and even a pink coral.

To protect this extremely rich intertidal community, the provincial government granted Race Rocks ecological reserve status in 1980. In 1998 the federal government attempted to further solidify this protected status by declaring Race Rocks one of four national Marine Protected Areas. Unfortunately in 2004 this had not yet been formally recognized; competing interests seem to have slowed progress. Eventually it is hoped that the 225 hectares (of which only 2 are terrestrial) will officially be managed for the purpose of conservation and education only. The light station, decommissioned in 1997, now serves as a research facility with arrangements for bookings handled by Lester Pearson College. Former lightkeepers live on site serving as island guardians. Check out the Lester Pearson College website for more information on Race Rocks or go to www.racerocks.com. Links will take you to an informative and up–to–date management plan for this area titled "Vancouver Island Region Management Plan for Race Rocks Ecological Reserve."

With all the protected status here a paddler may ask if recreational use is restricted. No it isn't, as long as we demonstrate low impact activities such as wildlife viewing, bird watching and photography. Although landing at Great Race is not encouraged without making prior arrangements, if you do choose to land simply inform the caretakers of your intentions.

The striking tower on Great Race was one of the first lighthouses on the BC coast. Made from metre–thick granite blocks that were precut, then

Paddler and the 140 year old lighttower on Great Race.
Photo: Bruce Holland.

shipped from Scotland, they were re-assembled in 1860. Over the next 140 years the lightkeepers here rescued many boats, but still over thirty–five vessels have met disaster in the vicinity of the rocks.

Unfortunately visits here are cut short as current speeds start to increase soon after slack. Return in good time to your launch at either Pedder Bay or Weir Beach.

4 Albert Head To Witty's Lagoon

Difficulty   Novice conditions – minimal risk
Distance   5 nmi round trip
Duration   Day trip
Chart   3440, Race Rocks to D'Arcy Island (1:40,000)
Tides   Reference Port: Victoria
      Secondary Port: Esquimalt
Currents   Reference Station: Race Passage
Camping   No camping
Land Jurisdictions   Department of National Defense – Albert Head Capital Regional
   District Park – Witty's Lagoon

The notable absence of housing is most refreshing, especially given this area's close proximity to a large centre. Views across Juan de Fuca Strait to the snow–capped Olympics enhance the entire route. Paddle through the quiet waters at Witty's Lagoon to the waterfall.

Paddling Considerations

Only when winds blow from the south is this area exposed. Currents are minimal—except at the entrance to Witty's Lagoon on the ebb.

It may not be possible to enter the lagoon by kayak during low tide because the waters at the entrance become too shallow to permit passage.

Novice paddlers will appreciate this route.

Getting There and Launching

This route is accessed from launches at either Albert Head or Tower Point.

To get to the Albert Head Lagoon launch from Victoria take the Old Island Highway (Highway 1A) then Sooke Road (Highway 14). Turn left at the Metchosin Road turn–off. Follow Metchosin Road to Farhill Road.

Turn left. Make another turn onto Park Drive and then right onto Delgada. Delgada terminates at Albert Head Lagoon Park where the beach launch is only a few meters away and vehicles can be left in an adjacent lot.

To access the Tower Point launch follow the previous launch directions to Metchosin Road. Follow Metchosin Road to Duke Road. Duke Road forms a loop, so proceed to the second junction of Duke Road with Metchosin Road (about 1 km, or 0.6 mi. past the first junction). Turn left and follow Duke Road to Olympic View Drive. At the bottom of Olympic View Drive is a steep staircase that leads to the beach launch. Parking is limited here, but for the shortest paddle to Witty's Lagoon this is the best launch.

The Route

This route is described assuming a launch from Albert Head Lagoon.

Albert Head Lagoon offers refuge to a variety of pelagic birds, but the most impressive among them are the mute swans. This is an introduced species—not to be mistaken for the native Trumpeter Swan. Originally

Gulls take flight in Witty's Lagoon. Photo: Maurice Robinson.

imported from Europe, they long ago escaped captivity and successfully bred in the wild.

Launch from the beach adjacent to the lagoon, and paddle toward Albert Head, an above–the–foreshore area that is owned by the Department of National Defence. The gunhousings, evident as you round the headland, were constructed in World War II. The enclosed artillery was apparently capable of lobbing shells across Juan de Fuca Strait. Today, the barracks are used during the summer for military training sessions. The nearby lighthouse was built after a huge ship, the Empress of Canada, went aground here in 1929.

Seal escort is almost guaranteed during circumnavigation of the Haystock Islets. In the surrounding shallows, abundant kelp and rocky ledges provide an ideal environment for these curious creatures. Onshore, river otter trails weave through the bramble. From a distance the thick undergrowth crowning the Haystocks gives the appearance of old–style haystacks. So strong is the resemblance that it leads to speculation that the islets were originally named "Haystack," but, in the process of chart creation, perhaps an "a" was mistaken for an "o."

Tower Point, part of Witty's Lagoon Park, has beaches on the west side that provide landings. Interestingly, this entire point presents some of the best North American examples of a geologic formation called pillow basalt. These rounded "blobs" of rock are created when lava flows from sea–floor rifts. Sea water contacting the molten rock cools it almost instantly into rounded shells. The material inside each pillow cools at a slower rate. Tower Point is a composite of pillow formations that formed some forty–five million years ago. The "pillows" are easily observed by paddlers all along the shore.

Enter Witty's Lagoon from the north end of the spit, a route that is easiest to negotiate when incoming flood tides overpower outflows from the lagoon. Passage to the lagoon may not be possible during very low tides. (There is a delayed reaction to tides within the lagoon. High tide occurs outside the lagoon sooner than it does inside.)

Stagnant waters, expansive mud beaches and a pungent fragrance are part of the highly productive marine environment at Witty's. Microscopic creatures especially adapted to low salt levels flourish in these seemingly deserted shores, providing abundant food for large crustaceans and in turn creating an invaluable feeding area for hundreds of shore birds including mallards, buffleheads, herons, Canada geese, sandpipers, yellowlegs and kingfishers.

The pilings found along the lagoon's north shore were put in place at the turn of the century when the fresh water required by families living out on Tower Point had to be brought in from a few kilometres away. Wood pipes lashed with wire and supported by pilings were part of the gravity–feed system that was installed. The rudimentary structure was apparently difficult to maintain, and freezing winter temperatures and summer droughts took their toll. The pilings are all that remain.

Paddle to the head of the lagoon to Sitting Lady Falls—most spectacular from winter to early summer. The falls are the result of a geologic process called "rebounding." As the weight of the ice was removed following the last glacial period, the land rebounded to former elevations. In the rebounding process, Metchosin Creek was left higher than it stood before the ice advanced. The falls are attempting to erode an even gradient back to the sea.

The Capital Region District park surrounding the lagoon is worth exploring. Described as a birder's paradise, over 160 bird species have been identified here including orange–crowned warblers and dark–eyed juncos. Trails follow the lagoon, lead up to the falls and pass through Douglas fir forests. A nature house just east of the falls, is open on weekends.

Heading to Albert Head from Witty's Lagoon. Photo: Maurice Robinson.

2 Oak Bay

It is hard to believe that a paddling experience of such high caliber can be had in such close proximity to a large urban centre. Within minutes of launching expect to be curiously eyed by the dozens of harbour seals that inhabit these waters. Pass by rocky islets that serve as nesting sites for the glaucous winged gull, cormorant, and black oystercatcher. All the while take in unobstructed views of Mount Baker and the Olympic mountains. In the morning explore the upper and middle reaches of the intertidal zone for blue mussels, acorn barnacles green anemones and purple stars.

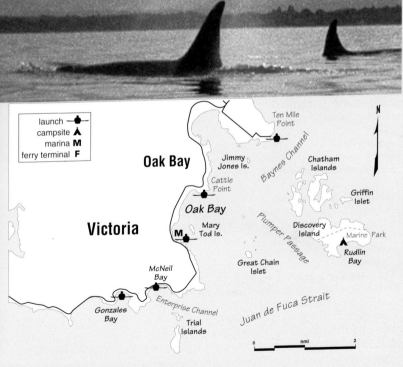

Photo: Kelly Irving.

5 Discovery and Chatham Islands

Difficulty Intermediate conditions, moderate risk
Distance 10 nmi – round trip circumnavigation of Discovery Island
6 nmi – circumnavigation of Chatham Island
Duration Day trip or overnight
Chart 3440 – Race Rocks to D'Arcy Island (1:40,000)
Tides Reference Port: Victoria
Secondary Port: Oak Bay
Currents Reference Station: Race Passage
Secondary Station: Baynes Channel
Camping Discovery Island BC Marine Park
Land Jurisdictions BC Parks – Discovery Island, Indian Reserves – Chatham and
Discovery Islands, Ecological Reserves – Great Chain Island and Chain islets,
Alpha Islet, Jemmy Jones Island and Ten Mile Point

Seasoned Victoria paddlers love this route. Within minutes of launching, they are treated to harbour seals, a sea bird colony and countless islets. Eventually they land on an uninhabited shore where hectares of fir and arbutus woodlands provide hours of exploring. An open field in a little–developed marine park provides for overnight camping. Views southward to the snow–capped Olympic Mountains or westward to Mount Baker further enhance this easily–accessed getaway.

Paddling Considerations

The currents in Plumper Passage and Baynes Channel demand careful consideration. They flow from 3 to 6 knots thereby demanding a crossing during minimum flows or, better yet, at slack. Determine slack water by referring to Baynes Channel, a Secondary Reference for Race Passage.

Expect tide rips during peak flows and, when wind and opposing currents meet, steep standing waves.

Although the area boasts predominantly calm days during the summer, strong southeasters ccan affect these routes; therefore listen to wind forecasts prior to heading out.

Because of the frequency of strong currents, the routes are not recommended for inexperienced paddlers.

Getting There and Launching

Paddlers coming from the Swartz Bay ferry terminal or from Highway 1 will head into the centre of Victoria along Blanshard Street. Turn left on Fort Street, and follow it to its "Y"–shaped intersection with Oak Bay Avenue. Follow Oak Bay Avenue to Newport Avenue. Turn right and follow Newport Avenue for a couple of blocks, then turn left on Windsor Road. In one block make another right onto Beach Drive. Public access to the water is located within a block of this last turn. Because the launch is on the opposite side of the road, you may choose to turn your vehicle around

Landing on Discovery Island at sunset. Photo: Andrew Madding.

to get as close as possible to the concrete access ramp.

The second launch at Cattle Point is accessed by continuing northward along Beach Drive to the sign indicating "Cattle Point Scenic Loop." Take the loop to access one of two boat ramps. There is ample parking.

The third launch is at Ten Mile Point's Smuggler's Cove, also known as Maynard Bay. Continue northward again, along Beach Drive, until it runs into Cadboro Bay Road. Follow Cadboro Bay Road past Cadboro Bay Village to Sea View Road. Turn right onto Sea View Road. It very quickly runs into Tudor Avenue. Follow Tudor Avenue to McAnally, then turn right again. Look for a beach in the elbow of a sharp left on this road. This is Smuggler's Cove. Leave vehicles at the side of McAnally Road, and launch from the adjacent shore.

The Route
Discovery Island

From the launch adjacent to the Oak Bay Marina, paddle past jetties and hundreds of sailing craft that moor in this protected bay. By hugging the western shores of Mary Tod Island, avoid confronting the marine traffic that enters the bay from the narrow south entrance.

All along the 2 nmi from Mary Tod to Discovery Island are low–tide rocks, tiny islets, offshore shallows and narrow passageways that cause increased tidal flows and, in some instances, tide rips. Although you can avoid most of the turbulence by crossing close to slack, be on the constant lookout for eddylines and the current flows that influence kayaking speed and direction.

The entire Chain Islets' archipelago will delight paddlers. Dozens of harbour seals, whose bobbing heads are often mistaken for the bulb of the giant bull kelp, are a constant presence here. Hundreds of glaucous–winged gulls make Great Chain their guano–splattered domain. Pelagic cormorants also take up residence, along with the black oystercatchers that prefer the low–tide rocks. Due to the sensitive nature of nesting birds, the entire island group is protected as an ecological reserve. Landing at any time is not permitted.

Discovery Island gets its name from the ship commanded by one of Vancouver Island's original explorers, Captain Vancouver. Chatham was named after the Discovery's consort. Neither of the ships came close to these islands because the expedition followed the continental shore, but the islands were named in their honour during a survey that took place almost sixty–five years later in 1846.

Begin a circumnavigation of Discovery Island by heading to any one of the large sheltered bays on the southwest shore that are within the Discovery Island Marine Park boundary. They serve well as a rest stop following the 2.5 nmi crossing from Oak Bay. Carry on with either a clockwise or counterclockwise paddle around Discovery. It is described here in a clockwise sequence.

Paddle the shallow channel between Chatham and Discovery Islands. Expect moving water at peak floods and ebbs—recognizing that

Native camp, west side of Discovery, early 1900s. Photo: Royal BC Museum.

Harlequin Duck

The seasoned Pacific coast paddler soon comes to recognize the mouse-like squeak of the Harlequin Duck. The same can not be said of east coast paddlers where the Harlequin is now endangered.

Named after Italian actors who wear a mask and dress in brightly painted costumes this is one of the most attractive of sea ducks. The male is particularly striking with his slate blue plumage, chestnut flanks and streaks of white on its head and body.

Also known as "sea mice" and "squeakers" the Harlequin is most likely to be found in the shallows over wave-pounded rocks and ledges. These little nodding birds have an extremely high metabolic rate and are constantly feeding, prying vast numbers of limpets, small crabs, chitons and mussels from rocky crevices.

Interestingly the Harlequin leaves the sea to breed – typically setting up a nest site in the spring beside fast-flowing streams. Difficult to locate these inland nests have been found under logs, in tree cavities and under bank overhangs. Within 24 hours of hatching the young Harlequins are led to the secluded stream where they quickly learn to feed on aquatic insects and larvae. They fly

Photo: Bob Davidson.

to their coastal environment several weeks later.

There are an estimated 200,000 to 300,000 Harlequins along the Pacific Coast whereas along the eastern Atlantic Coast fewer than 1,000 individuals remain. Historically this endangered east coast population was estimated at 5,000 to 10,000 birds. In Canada the Harlequin is protected from game bird hunting however the difficult to identify female is threatened by incidental shooting. Breeding sites are threatened as well with the creation of hydro electric dams – particularly on the east coast.

flows are fairly gentle and not nearly as complicated as those in Baynes Channel. The entire northern half of Discovery Island is reserve land and therefore private. The Songhees Band does not permit exploring ashore. Paddle mid channel taking in the magnificent little isles that lead to Griffin and Alpha Islets, or

on clear days an unobstructed view of Mount Baker.

Alpha Islet has been protected with ecological reserve status. More than sixty species of wildflowers grow here. Showy stands of camas, golden paintbrush, pink sea blush and chocolate lilies are prominent in spring. As the reserve has been established for the protection of this unique flora, observe this islet from the water.

Watch for increased flows in the approach to Seabird Point, take advantage of the close–to–shore backeddies and avoid occasional off-shore rips by hugging the coastline. The name of this point isn't taken from water birds but rather from a paddle steamer that caught fire here in 1858. Before she was completely consumed by the blaze, she apparent-ly ran aground to save those on board. The lighthouse was built in 1886. In the summer of 1996 this light station, manned for over one hundred years, became automated.

As the south shore of Discovery is open to prevailing south winds, it is necessary that paddlers check wind forecasts. However, even when seas are calm, there are hazards present that require mentioning. First, submerged rocks, particularly across the entrance to Rudlin Bay, along with adjacent shallows, do cause breakers. Second, the currents in this area are unpredict-able. Large backeddies cause flows that run in a direction opposite to what is expected. Finally, there are occasional rips off Commodore Point. These haz-ards, although worthy of note, are not always present. In fact, most days throughout the summer, paddling along the shores of Rudlin Bay is easy, safe and provides excellent access to Discovery Island Marine Park.

Paddlers will notice within 0.5 km (0.3 mi) of rounding Seabird Point a portal sign indicating that these lands are within Discovery Island Marine Park. The pebble beach here is ideal for landing. On the bench above this shore is an open field that provides ample designated camping space. A pit toilet, picnic tables and an information shelter are part of the development. A minimal fee for an overnight stay is charged. An honour payment system has been instituted with the construction of a self–regis-tration vault.

This has to be one of the most stun-ning of the Gulf Islands marine parks. The sweeping views over Juan de Fuca Strait across to the Olympic Mountains alone make a visit to this spot more than worthwhile. Onshore there is a trail system stretching from the Coast Guard light station to Commodore Point and across to the westernmost shores of the park. Wander through open meadowland or follow pathways shaded by a canopy of arbutus or Garry oak. Sheep have never grazed Discovery. Subsequently, the island has large numbers of plants not found on previously farmed islands like Port-land or Prevost. The floral presence is particularly noticeable in spring when the woodlands abound with the colour of blossoming wildflowers.

In the upper meadow explore the locale of the old home site of Captain Ernest Beaumont. For almost fifty years he and his wife lived on this island. Their beautiful home, long ago torn down, overlooked Rudlin Bay. The once–elaborate garden, complete with stone–lined ponds and fruit trees, although very overgrown, is still in evidence. Upon his death in 1967, the Captain left these 60 ha (150 ac) to the province. He is also responsible for do-nating the land on South Pender that make up Beaumont Marine Park.

Carry on your from–the–water circumnavigation of Discovery by

Camping on Discovery Island's Rudlin Bay. Photo: David Spittlehouse.

heading to the island's southwestern shores. Two or three sheltered coves found along this stretch may summon you ashore. Up until the early part of this century, the natives set up seasonal camps in this area.

From here paddlers may choose to either explore the waters surrounding the Chathams or return to Oak Bay via the Chain Islets.

The Chatham Islands

Both Chathams are private reserve lands, owned by the Victoria–based Songhees Band. Up until 1996 the natives granted public access to the islands. This changed due to increased concern brought about by careless visitors. Two fires, one in 1993, the other in 1996, led to an enforced public closure. The Songhees Band patrols the area during peak seasons and will ask those who land to move on.

However, I continue to include a description of the Chathams in this guidebook as the waterways that surround the islets are worth exploring. Let tidal flows assist you to determine a clockwise or counterclockwise route. The passes between the two Chathams and between Chatham and Discovery present stronger currents at peak floods and ebbs and, although generally manageable, an extra effort may be required by paddlers who find themselves in opposition to the flow. Crossing eddylines may also be necessary. The route will be described as a clockwise circumnavigation of the larger of the two Chatham Islands. From Discovery head toward the radio towers visible on Chatham's southwest shore.

On the eroded banks of large Chatham (just past the two radio towers) are two grave crosses dated 1917 and 1920.

One of the two natives buried here died at the age of twenty–three. According to the marker he was a chief.

Paddle the south side of the island past a tropical–looking sandy shore. Carry on to the eastern shore and a number of sheltered bays that look out to Haro Strait and the American San Juans. At low tide don't miss paddling close to this shoreline in order to take in a colourful and prolific intertidal zone. A meandering, mud–lined lagoon that cuts almost all the way through the island is accessed from this eastern shore. If water levels permit access (high tide only) this unique maritime environment is worth exploring. Large numbers of sea birds, including the heron, kingfisher and bald eagle, are commonly found. In the late afternoon and early evening, huge flocks of crows fly into the area. They are heading to roosting sites found on both Chatham and Discovery Islands.

Return to the lagoon entrance and round the island's northernmost tip. Increased flows and some turbulence are frequently found off the point. Listen for the mouse–like squeak of the brightly coloured Harlequin Duck as they search the rocky shallows for food.

Head to the sheltered cove on the northwest side of the island, a delightful nook that is popular with the Victoria yachting crowd. Carry on to the picturesque channel between the two Chathams. Here, grassy knolls and copper–barked arbutus line the shores of pebbled coves and quiet sheltered bays. Most enticing is a concealed lagoon, only accessible at high tides. Look for its narrow entranceway about halfway along the north shore of small Chatham. Inside this tiny enclave an overwhelming quiet prevails. Carry on with a return to the pass between Chatham and Discovery Islands and a re–linking with the Discovery route.

Access from Smuggler's Cove

Paddlers may access the Chatham and Discovery Islands from Ten Mile Point's Smuggler's Cove launch. (See the launches described at the beginning of this route.) The tiny islets at the entrance to Smuggler's Cove (also called Maynard Bay) have been declared an ecological reserve. Inhabiting the rock slopes are acorn barnacles, flat plate limpets and, in the cracks and crevices, tiny black periwinkle snails. Harder to see but also present are gumboot chitons, sea urchins, red sea cucumbers and purple ochre stars.

Immediately upon leaving the shelter of this marine–rich cove, paddlers are out in Baynes Channel, a stretch of water that is notorious for tide rips and standing waves. Schedule the crossing close to slack, or expect to be swept along by rushing, turbulent water. If you make a slack–water crossing, anticipate reaching Strongtide Island in about half an hour.

To the inside of Strongtide Island are tiny islets that are ideal for exploring. The narrow passageways form a kayaker's haven. At times of increased flow, the currents are ideal for practicing moving–water skills in slow–moving, protected waters.

Head to the channel between the two Chathams and link up with the routes described in the previous Chatham and Discovery Islands sections.

6 Trial Island

Difficulty Intermediate conditions – moderate risk
Distance 3 nmi round trip
Duration Half–day
Chart 3440 – Race Rocks to D'Arcy Island (1:40,000)
Tides Reference Port: Victoria
Secondary Port: Oak Bay
Currents Reference Station: Race Passage
Secondary Station: Baynes Channel
Camping No camping
Land Jurisdictions Ecological Reserve – Trial Island

Here is a route perfectly suited to an afternoon or evening paddle. Paddle to the islands for a gourmet picnic on the beach and return to the launch by sundown. Rare and endangered plant species thrive on these treeless isles. In spring the tiny blossoms present a colourful palate. In recognition of the ecological reserve status of this unique environment take in this natural beauty from the shore.

Paddling Considerations

Depending on the tides, currents of up to 3 knots can be expected between McNeill Bay and the Trial Islands and up to 6 knots off the outer shores of the islands. Eddies and fast–moving water are common. Of greater concern are the steep standing waves that are frequently encountered off the island's southwest corner. Schedule paddling in the area, and avoid most of the hazardous waters by paddling close to slack.

Because of the scheduling required, exposure to winds and the likelihood of difficult-to-handle waters, this route is recommended for experienced paddlers only.

Trial Island serves as a winter haul-out for California and Stellar sea lions. Photo: Andrew Madding.

Strong currents are often found in Enterprise Channel, so a launch from Gonzales Bay is recommended.

Getting There and Launching

To access the McNeill Bay launch out–of–towners enter Victoria via Blanshard Street. Continue along Blanshard, through the downtown area to Fairfield Road. Turn left onto Fairfield, and drive along its entire length until it becomes Beach Drive. Follow Beach Drive, and within a short distance, the sea will come into view. This is McNeill Bay. Park on Beach Drive. Launch from anywhere along the pebble beach.

To access the second launch on Gonzales Bay, enter Victoria via Blanshard Street and follow it until it eventually terminates and becomes Douglas Street. Follow Douglas southward to Dallas Road, then turn left. Follow Dallas Road along the seashore to the point where it runs into Crescent Road. Here there is a small park with a lot for vehicles. Park your car and walk down the concrete path to launch from Gonzales Bay's sandy beach.

The Route

The route is described here using the Gonzales Bay launch.

Gonzales Bay was originally named Foul Bay, but because of negative connotations, the residents petitioned for a name change. (A major roadway in the area bears the name Foul Bay.)

Tucked behind Harling Point and visible from the water is a Chinese cemetery. Before World War II, all Chinese immigrants were returned to their homeland to be buried, but because shipments occurred only once every seven years, bodies were kept waiting in a crypt in Victoria. When the Chinese government started refusing the remains, 849 Chinese were buried at this particular site (Wolferstan).

The flows get stronger during peak floods and ebbs as you get closer to McNeill Bay. Unless you are paddling at slack, avoid this faster–moving water by navigating directly toward the inside of the smaller of the two Trial Islands. Several pebble beaches that line the perimeter of this tiny isle are suitable for landing.

Trial Islands host several rare and endangered plant species. Plant species that have disappeared because of urban development still thrive on these isolated isles. Among the rare species represented are Macoun's meadow–foam, a plant that is extremely sensitive to environmental changes; the golden Indian paintbrush; the chick lupine, reported only in the Puget Sound area and found locally at Trial and Victoria's Holland Point; and the rosy–owl clover. Several other plant species that are almost as scarce grow in the area. Carolina foxtail, Henderson's checkermallow, bear's foot sanicle and the seaside lotus are but a few of these rarely seen plants (Ceska).

In the early 1990s these islands were rightly granted ecological reserve status. In order to protect the unique flora, restrict your stops to beaches and, in the spring, observe the blossoming wildflowers from the shoreline.

Continue a circumnavigation of large Trial Island by passing through the narrow channel between the two

Fast moving water along Trial Island's outer shoreline. Photo: Andrew Madding

islands. Strong winds, a 6–knot current and steep seas led to the 1906 installation of this light station. The lighthouse here continues to be staffed—in fact, it is the only lighthouse on the southern tip of Vancouver Island that has not become automated. The original lighthouse structure has long since been replaced, but the first lantern room and original lens are on display in Victoria's Bastion Square. For those interested in knowing more about the automation of lighthouses on the BC coast check www.fogwhistle.ca/bclights. It lists all the lighthouses that remain staffed along with those that have become automated.

Notice the rip symbols on the chart that indicate the likelihood of turbulence along Trial's outer shores. Other than at times that are close to slack, overfalls, eddies and fast–moving water (at times reaching 6 knots) are common all along this stretch. Conditions are made worse when winds oppose the current, and huge standing waves result. The worst of the maelstrom is found off the island's southwest corner.

Avoid the risks of paddling through such hazardous seas by scheduling a visit to this area. When conditions are right, get in close to the outer shoreline, one of the few stretches of coast in the Gulf Islands that supports a large number of gooseneck barnacles and California mussels.

Victoria's CFAX radio leases a section of Crown land on the island and has erected the towers that are an obvious presence on the west side. To the inside of the towers is a delightful beach appropriate for landing where you can stretch out onshore prior to returning to the Gonzales launch.

3 Sidney

It would be hard for a paddler to ever tire of this area. Year after year I head back to these waters to explore the countless miniature islets and miles of shoreline. The open water stretches are short. It is never long before the paddler is once again traveling along that interesting interface between the shore and the sea. It is common to observe harbour seals, otters, mink and eagles along these routes. And these islands have very interesting stories to tell – human history abounds here. This is an area that should not be missed.

Kayaks ashore on Portland Island. Photo: Kelly Irving.

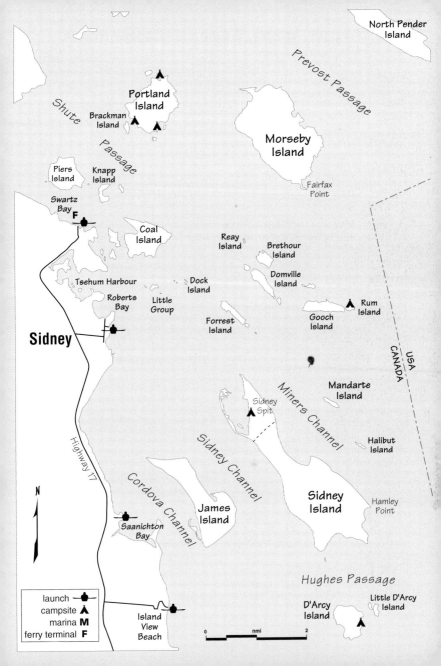

7 South Sidney – James, D'Arcy and Mandarte Islands

Difficulty Intermediate conditions – moderate risk
Distance 16 nmi round trip
Duration 2 – 3 days
Chart 3441, Haro Strait, Boundary Pass and Satellite Channel (1:40,000)
Tides Reference Port: Fulford Harbour
Secondary Ports: Saanichton Bay and Sidney
Currents Reference Station: Race Passage
Secondary Stations: Haro Strait (Hamley Point), Sidney Channel
Camping D'Arcy and Sidney Islands
Land Jurisdictions Gulf Islands National Park Reserve – D'Arcy and Sidney Islands
Indian Reserve – Mandarte Island

Paddlers who can get beyond the white–sand beaches on James Island will discover the many highlights along this route. Curiously eyeing passers–by are the harbour seals that frequent these waters. D'Arcy Island, now part of the Gulf Island National Park Reserve, was for years a desolate place where immigrant Chinese lepers spent their final years. Lesser visited than other Gulf Island parks, paddlers are more likely to find themselves the only ones onshore. Mandarte Island shouldn't be missed. Hundreds of nesting birds share every conceivable ledge on this rocky outcrop—along with the ramshackle bird blinds. Easily extend this trip by spending another night on nearby Sidney Island (see trip 8).

Paddling Considerations

This route is exposed to prevailing south winds, especially in the 3.5 mi stretch between the launch and D'Arcy Island.

Three–knot currents in both Cordova and Sidney Channels are occasionally met by opposing winds, thereby creating waves. Schedule paddling to avoid the strongest flows by referring to current references for Sidney Channel (on Race Passage) in the Tide and Current Table or by using the Current Atlas, both published by the Canadian Hydrographic Service.

Given the 3.5 mi crossing and the exposure to winds along this open stretch, this route is recommended for experienced paddlers.

Getting There and Launching

There are two launches for this trip —Island View Beach and Saanichton Bay. Both are located in Saanichton just north of Victoria.

Paddlers from the mainland dock at Swartz Bay, drive southward along Highway 17. Paddlers coming from Victoria head northward on Highway 17.

The Island View Beach launch is accessed by turning off Highway 17 onto Island View Road and following it to its seaward terminus. Launch from the ramp adjacent to Island View Beach Park. Although this is the easiest of the 2 launches for this trip

Launching from Island View Beach. Photo: David Spittlehouse.

there is no overnight parking here. The Saanichton Bay launch allows for overnight parking.

Launch from the government wharf on Saanichton Bay by turning off Highway 17 onto Mount Newton Cross Road. Within a block make a left onto Lochside Drive, then a right on James Island Road. The government wharf on Saanichton is found at the end of road. Leave vehicles in the nearby lot, and launch from the float at the base of the public wharf.

Allow fifteen minutes to reach the launch from Swartz Bay, about half an hour from Victoria.

The Route

With an overnight stay at D'Arcy Island this route could easily be paddled in 2 days. The trip could also be extended to 3 days by adding a night on Sidney Island.

The government wharf at Saanichton is reportedly the smallest public float on the BC coast. The float was originally used by Canadian Explosives Ltd. (now CIL) workers commuting the 1.5 mi to their workplace on James Island. From this launch head toward the southwest corner of James Island.

James Island

James Island is the only island in the Gulf Islands area that is completely surrounded by sand. The white beaches have attracted boaters for years, but up until recently landing was strictly forbidden by CIL. It purchased the island in 1913 and up until the 1970s used it as a location for its explosives plant. In the mid 1980s a clean–up program undertaken by CIL and the provincial government removed evidence of the years of industrial use. The island is private and in the 1990's had been purchased by a developer. Plans that included an exclusive village site, golf course,

Sidney – 61

stables and tennis courts ground to a halt. The current owner has managed to sustain the small golf course but apparently the island is once again for sale for considerable number of dollars. For now James is largely unused and intermittently inhabited.

Respecting that above high tide lines are private, pull up onto one of James Island's sandy shores. Considering that on a summer day the lure of sun and sand is sometimes overwhelming, this may be as far as you get! The small lagoon on the west side of James is particularly inviting with its shallow, calm waters.

The tusk of an Imperial mammoth was uncovered here half a century ago. Several specimens of Imperial mammoths have been uncovered in this area and in the gravel pits on the Saanich Peninsula. They have been dated from 17,000 to 20,000 years old.

D'Arcy Island's southern shore.
Photo: Andrew Madding.

The crossing from the south end of James Island over to Sidney Island is just over 1 nmi and is exposed to winds blowing up Haro Strait. As currents in the channel can reach up to 3 knots, consult the Current Atlas or the Tide and Current Tables for maximum flow predictions.

All of Sidney Island, except for the National Park Reserve on the north end, is private, owned by Sallas Forest Management. This interesting community manages a residential and sustainable forest management strata committed to preserving the island's natural features. You can check out their website at www.sidneyisland.ca

The distance from Sidney Island to D'Arcy is 1 nmi, and although currents in Hughes Passage tend to be minimal, they can increase to 2 knots during peak floods and ebbs. Harbour seals frequently haul out on exposed ledges near Sallas Rocks. This group of islets bears the name once given to Sidney Island.

D'Arcy Island

D'Arcy Island, a BC Marine Park from 1961 to 2003, is now part of the Gulf Islands National Park Reserve. Paddlers will relish these seemingly deserted shores. (The island is rarely visited by pleasure boaters as they seem to prefer the sheltered anchorages around Sidney Spit.) Make a stopover in a bay just north of the light on the west side of the island, and land near the visible remains of a concrete wall. This now–disintegrating building was once the caretakers house for the leper colony that operated on D'Arcy from 1891 to 1924. Little else remains of a thirty–year occupation by Chinese immigrants condemned to spend their final years on a lonely island in Canada.

Rich intertidal life abounds in the bay south of the light. Look into the low–tide shallows for colourful displays of purple stars, red sea urchins and an unusual seaweed, the iridescent algae. The iridescence is produced by an outer cuticle on the algae's fronds. The cuticle is comprised of laminated layers of cells, spaced in such a way that certain wavelengths of the spectrum are absorbed while others are reflected, thereby causing the iridescence.

Windswept trees clinging to a barren shoreline add to the desolate appearance of D'Arcy's south coast.

A Leper Colony

Leprosy was fairly widespread in the Orient at the turn of this century, and so occasionally Chinese immigrants entering Canada were infected with the dreaded disease. Because of the strict policies that demanded complete quarantine of such cases, the Canadian government set up two "lazarettos," one in New Brunswick, the other on the isolated shores of D'Arcy Island. Up until the completion of a recent archaeological study (1989), little was known of the living conditions of the handful of lepers living in exile on D'Arcy Island and nearby Little D'Arcy. They lived in almost total isolation. Food supplies were sent in only every three months, and until more frequent supplies were provided, it was necessary for the lepers to maintain a garden and keep chickens.

In 1905 C.J. Fagan, the province's Secretary to the Public Health Commission, visited the island. He wrote, "There was no pretension made to give medical treatment, and there is no effort made to relieve pain." He went on to recommend that "an effort be made to send the patients to some place where regular and systematic treatment is given."

The government did not follow his recommendations, but at some point a caretaker arrived and lived in the dwelling on large D'Arcy, and food supplies started to arrive weekly. The dilapidated concrete building that remains today was part of this one–and–a–half storey building containing five rooms and a porch and surrounded by a garden.

The rest is speculation, but there can be little doubt that those confined here had little to comfort them. In total exile, they were living away from all that was previously familiar to them. In 1924 the sole inhabitant was transferred to a new station on Bentinck Island, effectively terminating the thirty–three year existence of the D'Arcy Island colony.

Head to the more inviting camp location situated within a prominent sand–fringed cove. This formerly undeveloped site has facilities—including a half–dozen tent pads, picnic tables and pit toilets. It is not park's intention to "clip the wings" of those who seek a wilderness experience but rather to protect fragile environments from overuse. Respect efforts to lessen the impact of our presence and if you choose to spend the night here set up camp in designated areas.

A trail heads inland from this point. It crosses the island and then circumnavigates the island, passing by the ruins of the leper colony's caretaker's house.

You may find yourself looking enviably at the shores on Little D'Arcy where there is less undergrowth and more open areas. But Little D'Arcy is not part of the park. It is privately owned.

The Hughes Passage crossing from D'Arcy to Waymond Point on Sidney Island is 1 nmi. Park–like shores found on the east side of Sidney Island reward the paddler all the way to Hamley Point. Note that Hamley is a secondary current reference in the Tide and Current Tables.

Miners Channel was so named because it was part of the main canoe route used by miners heading to the Cariboo Gold Rush. There is occasional turbulence in the channel's shallower waters, especially when winds meet opposing tides. Halibut Island has little appeal except for a shell beach on its northern shore.

Mandarte Island

Mandarte Island is an Indian Reserve, shared jointly by the Tsawout and Tseycum First Nations. It is a fascinating island to paddle along. This massive bare rock is home to over fifteen thousand nesting birds, all of which fill the air with their raucous calls and pungent odours. Both pelagic and double–crested cormorants claim nesting sites here, with the double–crested dominating the higher elevations and the pelagic nesting on lower ledges. Pigeon guillemots nest under logs and in rock crevices, while glaucous–winged gulls lay claim to the grassy knolls and meadows. This island is also the only place on the inside passage where tufted puffins have been spotted. Their brightly coloured head and large bill on a black body are unmistakable. Perhaps of greatest interest are the various bird blinds constructed by aspiring ornithologists in their attempt to complete yet another study of life on the Mandarte colony. It is rumored there are more Ph.D.'s in zoology per acre on this island than on any other piece of real estate in the province.

After Mandarte, two route options are open to paddlers. The first option follows the route just described, only in reverse, omitting D'Arcy Island and returning to the Saanichton Bay launch. The return distance is 7 nmi.

The second option takes paddlers to either Sidney or Rum Islands, effectively linking this route with those described in the section on Central Sidney. The crossing from Mandarte to Rum Island is over 1.5 nmi. The distance from Mandarte to Sidney Spit is 2 nmi.

8 Central Sidney – Dock, Reay, Rum and Sidney Islands

Difficulty Intermediate conditions – moderate risk
Distance 11 nmi round trip
Duration 1 –2 days
Charts 3441– Haro Strait, Boundary Pass and Satellite Channel (1:40,000)
Tides Reference Port: Fulford Harbour
Secondary Ports: Saanichton Bay and Sidney
Currents Reference Station: Race Passage
Secondary Station: Sidney Channel
Camping Rum Island and Sidney Island
Land Jurisdictions Gulf Island National Park Reserve – Dock, Reay, Rum
and Sidney Islands

Miniature islets with secluded beaches are irresistible, and paddlers are sure to be captivated by those found all along this route. Don't miss the Little Group, Greig and Reay Islets with tiny pocket beaches hidden by drying reefs and rocky bluffs. Paddle on to Rum, an island gem that is part of the Gulf islands National Park Reserve. Walk along the sandy shores that surround Sidney Spit. Set up camp on the shores of a sheltered lagoon on Sidney Island or on the secluded shores of Rum Island.

Paddling Considerations
Expect currents of up to 3 knots around the islets within the Little Group and in the pass between these islets and the north end of Forrest. (Ebb flows are stronger than floods in this area.) Determine when to expect the stronger flows by referring to currents for Sidney Channel (on Race Passage) in the Tide and Current Tables or by looking at flows represented in the Current Atlas.

The area is exposed to winds that can blow from the southern quad-rants. Check wind predictions prior to launching.

Because it is likely paddlers will have to cross eddylines and paddle through moving water, and because the route is exposed to prevailing winds, it is not recommended for inexperienced paddlers.

Getting There and Launching
The launches for this route are located in Sidney, north of Victoria.

Paddlers from the mainland dock at Swartz Bay, drive southward toward Sidney on Highway 17. Paddlers coming from Victoria head northward to Sidney on Highway 17.

Drive to intersection of Highway 17 and Sidney's Beacon Avenue. Follow Beacon Avenue to Third Avenue, turn left then turn right off Third onto either Rothsay or Amherst Road. Both of these roads terminate at public beach accesses. Parking is available at the side of the road.

Allow fifteen minutes to reach the launches from Swartz Bay, about half an hour from Victoria.

Canada goose observing paddler's formation in channel off Dock Island. Photo: David Spittlehouse.

The Route

Because there is a notable similarity to all the buildings located along this shore, take note of surrounding landmarks so as to avoid confusion upon returning to the launch site. Cross over to Little Shell Island, the first islet in the Little Group, from either of the two launches. Beyond this point, expect tidal flows of up to 3 knots, especially on the ebb and when crossing from Kerr to Dock Island. Ideally, schedule paddling close to slack, or paddle with current flows.

Dock Island

Land on the pebble beach on the north end of Dock, one of several tiny islets in the southern Gulf islands that is now protected by its inclusion in the Gulf Islands National Park Reserve. Hike through scrubby Garry oak to the steep–sided inlet on the island's south shore. The Nonsuch, a replica of the Hudson's Bay Company's sixteenth–century, 8 gun ketch, used this location in 1972 to recreate the method used to haul a sailing ship out before docks were constructed, a procedure called careening. She entered the "dock" bow–first, with one side of her resting against logs that were propped vertically along the steep cliffs. During low tide, the crew scrubbed and painted the bottom of the ship. Graffiti, visible on a nearby rock face, commemorates the event. Limit your stay here to daytime and head to designated campsites on Rum or Sidney Islands.

~

Tidal flows between Dock and Forrest Islands can have a significant effect on paddling. If it isn't possible to paddle this section close to slack, watch for turbulence and eddylines, especially off the south end of Dock Island.

Don't miss a beautiful pebble beach in the sheltered cove on the northeast side of Forrest Island where it is possible to wander along the top of the nearby knoll and look out over the channel. Limit your exploration to below high tide lines, since the island is privately owned.

Passing Greig Island almost guarantees a glimpse of seals either hauled out on exposed reefs or swimming in the luxuriant kelp beds. Glaucous–winged gulls inhabit the treeless isle.

Reay Island
Head to Reay Island a tiny gem also now part of the Gulf Islands National Park Reserve. In the previous version of this guide I described Reay as an islet suitable for camping. In speaking to Parks Canada about their management plan for this islet in the fall of 2003, they indicated that they had made it a priority to look at current camping activity along the various kayak routes within this area in order to determine where to set up camp locations that will have the least impact on natural and cultural features. Until they have a look at this, and I did understand they were committed to doing so very quickly, I would encourage paddlers to limit stop–overs to daytime. The rewards of a visit to this tiny islet are plentiful. Either of the two sheltered coves provides suitable landings. Take in panoramic views of Boundary Pass and Mount Baker. Observe resident harbour seals, or simply relax on the secluded pebble beaches. And please, light no fires on this tinder–dry islet. A single errant spark in the early 1990s caused much damage here.

~

In the pass between Brethour and Domville Islands, gently sloping sandstone shelves rise to arbutus groves on the rocky ledges above. Both islands are private. Brethour Island's owners have posted a unique sign indicating a concern for trespassers. It reads, "Caution—Bull At Large." Domville Island boasts two beautiful beaches separated by a low gravel bar on its narrow south end.

The obvious presence of summer residences on Gooch and Comet Islands reveals the private status of these spots, yet an expansive shell and gravel beach on Comet will likely attract paddlers who require a short–term stopover. For an appropriate camp location, paddle on to Rum Island, watching for moderate current flows in the shallows east of Comet Island.

Rum Island
Rum Island is truly a Gulf Island's gem. The name "Rum" is derived from its use during the 1920s by rumrunners who needed a stepping stone for transporting prohibited spirits into the United States. (The island is less than a mile from the US border.) More recently, Rum Island was used as a summer residence by Mrs. McCaud–Nelson, a lover of wildflowers. Upon her death in 1978, the island was donated to the province to become a provincial park. At her request, the park was named Isle de Lis (Island of Lilies). Wildflowers, including the chocolate lily, continue to grace this tiny isle in spring. In 2003, Isle

Where Are the Blues?

Photo: Bob Davidson.

The great blue heron is never far from its nesting colony (heronry). Forty colonies support the estimated 1500 pairs found in the Strait of Georgia. Of these forty colonies only five have over a hundred nests: Point Roberts, University of British Columbia, Chilliwack, Mary Hill, Alouette Lake and Saltspring Island. The remaining coastal herons nest in small colonies or as solitary pairs and typically relocate their nesting sites every few years.

Great blue herons return to their natal nesting site in late February from locations that are most often within a 25 km radius of the colony. Monogamous pairs head to their treetop nest where in April they lay four eggs that hatch in May. During the next three weeks, parents must undertake the monumental task of feeding four insatiable mouths. Some chicks die of starvation while others, weakened by the intense competition for food, are pushed out of the nest. Miraculously, two or three will live long enough to fly away on their own. Survival remains precarious. Almost 75 percent of the young will not live beyond the first year because the demands placed upon the young birds are immense. Very quickly, they must develop the lightening-precise skills that are necessary for them to catch the large numbers of fish that ensure their survival.

The heron's key feeding areas are the eel grass beds. In fact they are so fundamental that biologists have concluded that herony size is proportionate to the size of the eel grass beds closest to the colony. Large beaches at the mouth of the Fraser River estuary support hundreds of pairs of herons, whereas the smaller beds on Vancouver Island support only a few hundred herons in total. The eel grass beds found in Sidney Lagoon once supported a now abandoned forty–five–pair colony.

Great blue herons are extremely shy birds, a characteristic that frequently works against them in breeding season. If a colony is sufficiently disturbed the nervous parents will leave the entire colony en masse. This phenomenon presents a pressing conservation issue for the blue heron. Landscapes that currently support heronies need to be managed to provide for heron needs during the critical nesting season. Herons are also prey of a growing eagle population that is now recovering from the effects of DDT contamination of the past century. Eagle predation on heron colonies could well result in herons seeking new nesting sites in other wooded areas, often where people also reside.

For more information on heron populations in this region and related conservation issues follow links specific to Rob Butler on the Environment Canada website at www.ecoinfo.ec.gc.ca or the Heron Working Group website at www.sfu.ca/biology/wildberg/hwg/abouterons.html.

The Great Blue Heron by ornithologist, Rob Butler also provides good information.

de Lis Marine Park was incorporated into the National Park Reserve. Parks Canada will continue with managing this park for overnight use.

Land kayaks on an easily accessed gravel isthmus linking Rum and Gooch Islands. Hike up the headland of Rum Island to access the half–dozen designated camp sites. In order to preserve the island's fragile environment, tenting is understandably restricted to the designated tent platforms. Fires are prohibited. A self–registration vault accepts the minimal fee charged per camping party. Picnic tables and sanitary facilities are also part of the development on Rum.

Paddlers who choose to make Isle de Lis a destination will not be disappointed. A cross–island trail terminating at Tom Point leads through the open forests and offers spectacular views of Haro Strait, Boundary Pass and the San Juan Islands. The distant droning heard from any vantage on Rum is from the light station on Turn Point. It warns of strong tide rips off the western point of Stuart Island in the American San Juans.

Watch for the swift currents that swirl through the kelp off Tom Point when paddling around to the south side of Rum and Gooch Islands. Note that the shallows of North Cod Reef can generate turbulence during peak floods and ebbs. This stretch of coastline is also exposed to prevailing south winds.

At this point, paddlers can extend this trip by linking up with Trip 7, or return to the Sidney launch site via Sidney Spit. The crossing from Gooch Island to Sidney Spit is about 2 nmi.

Paddlers on gravel beach linking Rum and Gooch islands. Photo: David Spittlehouse.

Sidney Spit

Notice the pilings driven into the sand bar at Sidney Spit. Apparently, the north end of the spit is gradually disappearing, so pilings were put in place to prevent further erosion. In his cruising guide Wolferstan appropriately describes this "valiant effort worthy of King Canute."

Sidney Spit offers the most popular of all the Gulf Islands anchorages. The wharf and mooring buoys quickly fill with pleasure boats. Onshore are numerous campsites, picnic tables, a large kitchen shelter and several pit toilets. Formerly Sidney Spit Marine Park, all 120 ha (300 ac) are now part of the Gulf Islands National Park Reserve.

Campground at Sidney Spit. Photo Gary Doran.

Paddlers may choose to pass by this busy north end and head to the quiet lagoon south of the spit where there is a huge meadow with plenty of designated camp space. A minimal camping fee is charged. A turn–of–the–century brick mill operated on these lagoon shores and at its peak employed about seventy men. Bricks from Island Brick and Tile Limited were used in the construction of Victoria's Empress Hotel. The various hollows that are found in the surrounding area show where clay was once scraped from the surface. Blackberry lovers will marvel at the heavily loaded bushes that now cover the hilly terrain.

Plan an inland excursion. The fallow deer that were introduced to James Island in the early 1900s swam to this island in the 1960s. Their escalating numbers will likely present a challenging conservation issue to the designated decision makers within the national park system.

It is probable that within the sheltered lagoon, visiting paddlers will see at least one, if not several, great blue herons. Home to these birds is close to where they can find food and where there is an appropriate nest site. Sidney Spit is an ideal environment for the great blue heron.

The distance from Sidney Spit to the Sidney launch is 2.5 nmi, and although currents in this section of the channel are minimal, paddlers may wish to coordinate this northward paddle with a flood tide. (There is a current reference for Sidney Channel on Race Passage.) One final bit of advice—watch for boat traffic as these waters are busy with pleasure craft.

9 North Sidney – Portland, Russell and Moresby Islands

Difficulty Beginner conditions – low risk
Distance 7 nmi – Portland Island round trip (add 2 nmi if using Sidney launches)
                10 nmi – Portland, around Moresby Island and return to launch
                10 nmi – Portland Island and Russell Island round trip
Duration 1 – 2 days
Chart 3441, Haro Strait, Boundary Pass and Satellite Channel (1:40,000)
Tides Reference Port: Fulford Harbour
            Secondary Ports: Sidney and Swanson Channel
Currents Reference Station: Race Passage
               Secondary Station: Sidney Channel
Camping Portland Island – Arbutus Point, Princess Bay and Shell Beach
Land Jurisdictions Gulf Islands National Park Reserve – Portland and Russell Islands,
Ecological Reserve – Brackman Island

The highlight of this trip has to be Portland Island. Over 200 ha (540 ac) of relatively undeveloped parkland are easily accessed by cross–island trails. Wander through overgrown meadows, apple orchards, blackberry thickets and beautiful dry coastal woodlands. Among the offshore islets, a glimpse of playful river otters and shy harbour seals is virtually guaranteed.

Spend an extra day and check out the interesting history of Hawaiian settlement on Russell Island. Or add yet another day to explore the little pocket shaped beaches on Moresby Island.

Paddling Considerations

Only in Moresby Passage do currents reach 3 knots, a passage that is easily avoided unless paddlers are heading to Moresby Island.

Winds in the area are usually light during the summer, with prevailing winds blowing from south quadrants.

The route around Portland Island and out to Russell Island is well suited for novice paddlers. As the distances are longer around Moresby Island novice paddlers may want to consider joining with intermediate paddlers.

Getting There and Launching

The launch from the government wharf adjacent to the Swartz Bay ferry terminal allows paddlers from the mainland to leave vehicles at Tsawwassen and walk kayaks onto the ferry. Upon arriving at the terminal ask ferry personnel to direct you to the gated exit on the eastern perimeter of the terminal. Bear to the left following the roadway. The government wharf launch at the bottom of Barnacle Road quickly comes into view. Launch from the beach to the left of the wharf. The walking distance from the ferry to the launch is about 0.5 km (0.3 mi).

Paddlers getting to this area via Victoria can access this same launch by following Highway 17 to the Swartz Bay ferry terminal. Take the "CPR Cargo and Canoe Cove" exit just before the terminal entrance. Go straight through at the lights and follow Dolphin Road around to Barnacle Road. A government wharf is located at the terminus of Barnacle Road. Launch from the beach adjacent to the wharf. However be aware that all adjacent parking space is often taken during the summer months.

Better launches, from a parking perspective, are those described for Trip 8 (off of Rothsay and Amhert Roads in Sidney.) Refer to the launches for trip 8, Central Sidney.

The Route
Portland Island

The route is described from the launch near the Swartz Bay ferry terminal .

For paddlers launching from Rothsay or Amherst Roads, paddle across the entrance to Roberts Bay and Tsehum Harbour. Head to Curteis Point and into John Channel between Coal and Fernie Island. Be aware that many pleasure craft ply these waters accessing Tsehum Harbour marinas. Be aware too that current flows in John Channel can be strong enough to slow progress. Add a couple of miles to the Portland Island paddle if you approach this route from these launches.

For paddlers using the Swartz Bay launch be aware that ferry–generated surf occasionally dumps in on this beach. Avoid a bad start by putting into the water after ferries have docked. Navigate toward Knapp Island.

Ferries are a major consideration in this area, especially in the summer. The large ferries arriving at Swartz Bay from the mainland use Colburne Passage between Knapp and Coal Islands. They move through the passage quickly. Do not make the crossing to Knapp unless the coast is clear.

Author dog-paddling to Portland Island.
Photo: Kathy Snowden.

Before leaving Colburne Passage, look over to Piers Island. Although the developed shores on this tiny isle are of little interest to paddlers, the island itself has an interesting history. Over six hundred Doukhobours, convicted of parading in the nude, were imprisoned on the island in 1932. A barbed–wire fence separating the men from the women ran down the centre of the island. By 1934 the nearly eight hundred prisoners were released (Wolferstan).

Paddle along the south shore of Knapp Island, and peer into the clear shallows to see the hundreds of clam shells that litter the ocean floor. The fortunate owners of this island have developed several wharves, a covered

Who Was "One–Arm" Sutton?

The name "One–Arm" was given to General Frank Sutton, who lost a limb during a bloody battle at Gallipoli in 1915. As the story goes, Sutton led five men into a shell hole, and when a hand grenade was hurled their way, Sutton tossed it back. He did the same with a second one, but only after he caught it in mid air. On the next try, he was not so lucky. The third missile exploded, shredding his arm. Sutton spent the remainder of the war designing weapons, then returned to his family in Shanghai.

In China he rose quickly to the rank of General—only one of three Europeans to receive the honourable position. Generous salaries and the royalties he received from his patented weaponry made him a wealthy man. And as if life wasn't going well enough, he won a $150,000 sweepstake, a windfall that allowed him to pursue a lifelong dream—the raising and training of thoroughbred horses.

Upon arriving in Vancouver in 1927, he bought a farm, a plane, some placer claims, Vancouver's Rogers and Mutual Life buildings and Portland Island. But the Depression struck and Sutton slid so far into debt that in desperation he took a job as a barker. By selling his assets he was able to salvage some money and returned to China where he worked as a correspondent for Hearst Publications. Soon, he was off again, this time to Korea. For some reason he was thrown out of the country and arrived in Hong Kong to news that the mortgage on Portland Island had been foreclosed.

He was well on the way to yet another fortune when the Japanese overran Hong Kong, and Sutton was placed in a prison camp where he died at age sixty. (Chettleburg)

moorage dock and a magnificent boat house, complete with a marine ways, on the shores of Trader Bay.

While crossing from Knapp to Hood Island (a tiny islet off the southern end of Portland Island), expect minimal currents. Rarely do the currents exceed 1.5 knots. From a distance Hood Island appears connected to Portland, but in fact it isn't. Paddle the narrow passage between the two islands, and enter Princess Bay on the south end of Portland Island.

Up until 1958 Portland Island was privately owned, but it went to the province when it was exchanged by then–owner Gavin Mouat for some timber rights. The entire 180 ha (450 ac) became a park when Princess Margaret returned the island to British Columbians in 1961 after receiving it as a gift on her Royal Visit in 1958. In appreciation, this island park was named "Princess Margaret Marine Park." Now part of the Gulf islands National Park Reserve, this is one of the parks where paddlers pay a nominal fee for an overnight stay. Overnight stays are limited to one of three designated camping areas where there are sanitary facilities—at Princess Bay, Arbutus Point and Shell Beach. Water is currently available from a mid–island pump. To determine its location, see information shelters at any one of the designated camp locations. It should however be noted that all water sources on national park reserve lands are under constant evaluation as a result of more stringent national water quality guidelines. Some of the wells may be capped. As always, it is best to bring your own water.

Heading to Arbutus Point on the north end of Portland Island. Photo: Bob Davidson.

Land in Princess Bay to access the weathered remains of an old orchard. In the fall the blackberry bushes here are loaded with ripened fruit. Walk inland through untended pastures to an open meadow where past owner "One–Arm" Sutton built a barn for his thoroughbreds. In 1989 a large herd of domestic sheep considered to have gone wild was removed by the then stewards, BC Parks. I have noticed since then a return of some of the wildflowers that likely grew in greater abundance prior to the years of constant grazing. Explore the island further by following any number of trails that both cut across and circumnavigate the island. Set up camp in the meadow nearest the old orchard, and look out over the bay's aquamarine waters to the Tortoise Islets, or return to your boat to

continue on with an exploration of Portland's magnificent shoreline.

From Princess Bay head northward past the Pellow Islets, travelling along what I'm convinced is the prettiest stretch of Portland's coastline. Arbutus and Douglas fir, sandstone beaches and grassy headlands line the entire shore. Frequently visiting the offshore islets are several river otter. Only once in all of the times I have paddled there have I not seen these playful creatures.

As tempting as some of the headlands along this stretch appear, camp in designated areas only. It is Park's intention to protect these fragile environments from overuse. They need our cooperation to do so.

In August of 1991 the MV Church was sunk off the Pellow Islets so it could serve as an artificial reef. The 53 m– (174 ft–) long coastal freighter was thoroughly cleaned. Holes were cut into the hull to allow diver access. As the ship has settled it has been colonized by anemones, sponges and various marine organisms, thereby establishing a very attractive, and now well used, dive site.

Continue on to Portland's north tip, known locally as Arbutus Point and undoubtedly the island's prettiest camp location. A crushed–shell beach provides access to a spacious level area nestled in under the arbutus canopy. A magnificent 180–degree view that encompasses Saltspring's Fulford Harbour, Pender and Moresby Islands and, off in the distance, Rum Island is the reward of all who camp here. On a clear day, Mount Baker's glacier–covered peak breaks the skyline. This is the sunrise and sundown side of Portland, and views of both are fantastic. There's an unusual sand beach nearby, backed by a narrow strip of midden that encloses a tiny salt marsh. Paths from here connect up with trails that encircle the island.

Parks has established facilities here, including several designated campsites, pit toilets and an information shelter. A self–registration vault and our honour assures the collection of a very reasonable, per person, camping fee.

Continue shoreline exploration by entering the waters in Satellite Channel. This is the side of Portland where the large ferries pass by on their run between Tsawwassen and Swartz Bay. For some paddlers, ferry swell means fun as attempts to surf on the rolling waves are made. Others are horrified by the erratic seas that are generated when the swell breaks onshore. Swing well out from major headlands to avoid these turbulent waters, and if you do land, pull boats up high onshore to avoid empty cockpits being filled with water.

From Arbutus Point paddlers may choose to make the 1.5 nmi crossing to Russell Island, another of the islands recently incorporated into the Gulf Islands National Park Reserve. See the next section in this route description for details.

Just south of Chad Island is a particularly inviting bay, easily distinguished from others by a high knoll that flanks its northern shore. From here, walk inland through the woodlands to a hand pump that provides fresh water. Those who choose to walk farther will discover that the open fields eventually lead to the previously described Princess Bay.

Kanaka Bluff points back to a time in history when native Hawaiian Islanders inhabited these shores. Both "Kanaka" and "Pellow" are the anglicised versions of original Hawaiian names.

South of Kanaka Bluff is the last, although certainly not the least, of Portland's camping areas. Land anywhere on the shell beach to access a level area that is large enough to accommodate several tents. Select a spot where the surrounding arbutus will shelter your campsite. Native peoples once camped here, as is evident by the midden that lines this entire shore.

Until recently, Brackman Island was private land. In 1989 it was designated ecological reserve status in order to protect its virtually undisturbed 4 ha (11ac). In 2003 it became a part of the Gulf Island National Park Reserve. Unlike all other Gulf Islands, Brackman has never been inhabited, logged or grazed, so several species of plants unique to our dry coastal ecosystem grow here. Douglas fir trees more than 250 years old and 13 plant species that are considered rare are found here. Magnificent kelp beds off the south tip of the island are also included in the reserve. Parks intends to maintain restricted access to this unique representative of Gulf Island vegetation. Admire this little isle from sea level.

On the return to Swartz Bay, avoid ferry traffic that occasionally passes through Gosse Passage by paddling between Knapp and Pim Islands.

Russell Island

The quickest way to get to Russell Island from this route is by crossing Satellite Channel from Arbutus Point on the north tip of Portland Island. BC Ferries frequent this channel—calculate your departure recognizing that ferries leave Swartz Bay on the odd hours from 7 am to 9 pm and every hour during peak summer months.

Russell Island was purchased in 1998 under the initiative of the Pacific Marine Heritage Legacy. In 2003 this 16 hectare (40 acre) island became a part of the Gulf Islands National Park Reserve.

In the late 1800s Hawaiians, also known as Kanakas, settled on several Gulf Islands including Portland, Saltspring and Russell. Skilled seamen and trappers, they came to this area as employees of the Hudsons

Early Hawaiian Settlers on the Southern Gulf Islands

Surprising to most there was a notable Hawaiian presence in the Gulf Islands dating back to the nineteenth century. Originally hired by the Hudson's Bay Company as labourers the Hawaiians soon became known for their abilities with language eventually working as language interpreters between fur traders and First Nations people. (Murray)

One of the most well known of the several hundred Hawaiians to arrive to the Pacific Northwest was William Naukana—selected to work for the HBC in 1840. After completing his service Naukana returned to Hawaii only to discover that his family's land had become a sugar plantation. He returned to the Pacific Northwest. Originally settling in the San Juan Islands, Naukana later moved to the Portland Island when the San Juans were ceded to the United States.

Several Hawaiian families settled at Isabella and Beaver Points on southern Saltspring Island, Portland, Coal and Russell Islands. Short distances between the islands and easy access allowed Hawaiian families to maintain close relationships. Traditional luaus were held at William Naukana's Portland Island house as well as Maria Mahoi's Russell Island home. Hawaiians from the local area would come for music, dancing, and seafood steamed on the beach. (Barman)

Another touchstone for the Hawaiian families in the area was St. Paul's Catholic Church in Fulford Harbour. Hawaiians contributed to its construction, were married and buried there. Today a small tribute to these families, a plaque,

Landing on Russell Island. Photo: Bob Davidson.

Bay Company. William Huamea and Maria Mahoi once owned Russell. The old house and orchard that remain today date back to the early 1900s. They stand as one of the few remaining Kanaka homesteads in the Gulf Islands.

The shoreline on Russell that faces Portland is steep and offers no suitable landings. In spring the violet–green swallows nesting in these south facing cliffs entertain passersby with their acrobatic flight. An obvious sandy beach on the west corner of the island provides a suitable landing where park's interpretive signs mark the start of a 20 minute loop trail. Wander through Douglas fir and Garry oak forest and along the rocky south facing shoreline.

Parks Canada has recognized the potential to interpret the Hawaiian presence here and at the time of this writing (2003) consideration was being given to do so. In the meantime the heritage buildings on Russell will likely be off limits to visitors.

Moresby Island

The quickest way to get to Moresby is by crossing Moresby Passage from the Pellow Islets on the northwest corner of Portland Island. As currents in the pass can reach 3 knots, schedule your crossing to avoid the stronger tidal flows.

Harbour Seals

Undoubtedly, the harbour seal is the most common marine mammal viewed by paddlers on the Pacific coast. We've all seen them—those curious creatures bearing a remarkable resemblance to cats in wetsuits that inspect our passing with large inquisitive eyes. We've seen them stretched out on exposed sandbars and rock ledges, and we have sent them scurrying for the water as we approach their favourite haul–out.

Seals have not always been so plentiful along this coast. They were once hunted for their pelt and killed for bounty, but since 1970 they have been protected, and healthy populations are approaching historic levels.

Special adaptations allow these incredible creatures to live almost entirely in the sea. To facilitate dives lasting up to twenty minutes, the heartbeat slows, body temperature drops and blood flow is reduced to all but essential organs. Pupils dilate to permit vision at depths of up to 600 m (1900 ft), and thick layers of blubber allow for swimming in water temperatures that seldom exceed 15°C (59°F). Even the newborn seal is ready for life at sea as pups are born fully furred and able to swim. Paddlers are occasionally alarmed to find seemingly abandoned newborns, but the pups are not orphaned. The mother has merely left her young while she feeds herself. Some 2 – 3 kg (4 – 7 lb) of fish are consumed daily by an adult seal, yet how much of this amount is salmon remains a controversial issue. Fishermen claim seals significantly deplete commercial salmon stocks, yet research indicates that most of the diet is comprised of smaller rockfish and smelts.

Photo: Sherry Kirkvold.

Some might describe Moresby Island as not worth the paddle. However, there are several features that make a visit to this distant isle worthwhile. What first drew me was the island's intriguing history. In the late 1800s, Captain Horatio Robertson left China and built two three– storey octagonal towers—one for his eight sons, the other for himself, his wife and three daughters—on Moresby Island. A 30 m– (100 ft–) long glass–covered balcony linked one tower to the other. While visiting Victoria, the Captain rode in a rickshaw pulled by his Chinese servants. Apparently he was very strict with his servants and his somewhat ruthless behaviour forced two of them to escape Moresby Island on a log raft. Nearly dead, they were picked up after several days at sea near Trial Islands (Wolferstan).

Unfortunately, Robertson's extravagant lifestyle is not in evidence today. Since the early 1900s, Moresby Island has been the site of a prosperous farm operation which is visible in the bay on the island's west side.

Navigate toward the sandy bay inside of Reynard Point to view one of the prettiest farms in all the Gulf Islands. A beautiful meadow, pungent with the smell of clover in the spring, adds to the pastoral setting. Although the presence of a private home discourages landing here, paddle the perimeter of the bay where great blue herons fish in the muddy shallows.

Paddle around Reynard Point to access Moresby's western shore where "U"–shaped coves are bound to lure you ashore. Spend a couple of hours stretched out in the sun on one of the secluded bays.

Fairfax Point is an absolute gem. Several pocket beaches that surround this southern tip offer spectacular views across Boundary Pass. Arbutus trees grace the entire area with their unusual copper–coloured bark, and in the spring a yellow flower brightens the personality of the otherwise spiny prickly pear.

~

Return to the Swartz Bay launch by crossing Prevost Passage and passing tiny Imrie Islet. Isolated from predators such as the raccoon and otter, this barren isle is used as a nesting site by the glaucous–winged gull. During a recent visit, I was impressed by the flock's harried response to the one predator that can access these shores—the bald eagle. What caught my attention was hundreds of gulls suddenly taking to the air. Within moments the raptor appeared. It seemed there was little the frenzied parents could do except emit their raucous call and circle about in confusion. Only the northwestern crows harassed the unwelcome visitor.

Upon approaching Coal Island, paddlers may feel the effect of tidal flows, especially on the ebb. Swing well out from Charmer Point as this is where flows will tend to be the strongest. Follow the steep–sided shoreline on the north side of Coal, and watch for strong flows again while crossing from Coal to Goudge Island and from Goudge Island to Swartz Head. Perhaps a greater hazard is the large number of pleasure boaters who use the two passes. Be conspicuous, as these boats often move quickly.

Dressed for a winter paddle, Portland Island.
Photo: Bob Davidson.

4 Saturna, South Pender and the Belle Chain Islets

This area takes paddlers into waters surrounding Saturna, the lesser inhabited of the southern Gulf Islands. There is a tremendous natural beauty here—sculpted sandstone cliffs, sandy shores and distant snow–capped mountains provide a photographic backdrop to a day on the water. Strong tidal flows bath the shallows with a plankton rich soup supporting a varied and colorful intertidal display. River otter, mink, harbour seals and the Stellar sea lion are present in large numbers. However the highlight that is sure to delight to the greatest degree is the sighting of a pod of orca whales. Quite simply, this area is a "must do."

Shoreline fronting campsites at Bedwell Harbour. Photo: Andrew Madding.

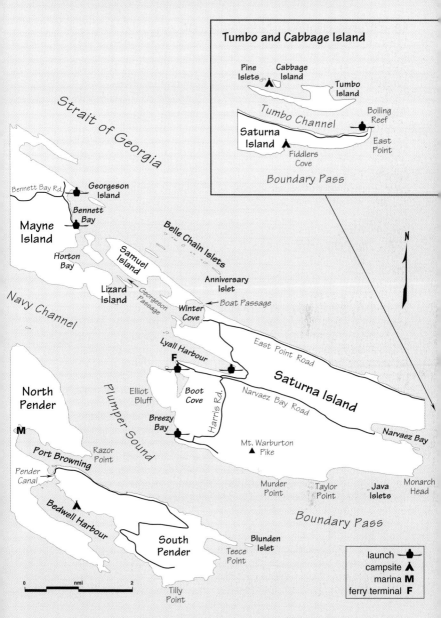

Tumbo and Cabbage Island

Pine Islets
Cabbage Island
Tumbo Island
Tumbo Channel
Boiling Reef
Saturna Island
East Point
Fiddlers Cove
Boundary Pass

Strait of Georgia

Bennett Bay Rd.
Georgeson Island
Bennett Bay
Mayne Island
Horton Bay
Samuel Island
Belle Chain Islets
Lizard Island
Georgeson Passage
Anniversary Islet
Winter Cove
Boat Passage

Navy Channel

Lyall Harbour
East Point Road
Saturna Island

North Pender
Elliot Bluff
Boot Cove
Narvaez Bay Road
Plumper Sound
Breezy Bay
Harris Rd.
Mt. Warburton Pike
Narvaez Bay

Port Browning
Razor Point
Pender Canal
Bedwell Harbour
South Pender
Murder Point
Taylor Point
Java Islets
Monarch Head
Boundary Pass

Blunden Islet
Teece Point
Tilly Point

0   nmi   2

launch ⚓
campsite ▲
marina M
ferry terminal F

Saturna, South Pender and the Belle Chain Islets – 81

10 Saturna Island Circumnavigation

Difficulty Intermediate conditions – moderate risk
Distance 18 nmi round trip
Duration 2 –3 days
Charts 3441 – Haro Strait, Boundary Pass and Satellite Channel (1:40,000)
Tides Reference Ports: Fulford Harbour and Point Atkinson
Secondary Ports: Narvaez Bay, Samuel Island South Shore
and Tumbo Channel
Currents Reference Stations: Race Passage and Active Pass
Secondary Stations: Boundary Passage and Boat Passage
Camping Cabbage Island and Saturna Island – Fiddler's Cove
Land Jurisdictions Gulf Islands National Park Reserve – Cabbage and Tumbo
Islands, Narvaez Bay and Taylor Bay, Indian Reserve – Fiddler's Cove

Saturna Island is the least populated of all the major Gulf Islands. It is largely undeveloped—an appealing attribute as so many of Saturna's shores remain undeveloped and now over 1100 ha (2700 ac) of the island are protected with National Park Reserve status. Paddle the open waters in the Strait of Georgia, and enjoy breathtaking views of Mount Baker. Enter the aquamarine waters around Cabbage Island, and camp in the arbutus woods. Round East Point where houses are so few or so well hidden that these shores appear uninhabited. Paddle under magnificent sandstone cliffs, explore the sheltered shores at Fiddler's Cove and Narvaez Bay, all the while watching for pods of orca out in Boundary Pass—a highlight that truly surpasses them all.

Paddling Considerations
Tidal streams in Boat Passage and around East Point demand consideration. Flows in Boat Passage reach up to 7 knots, and at East Point as well as adjacent Boiling Reef, they reach

upward of 5 knots. Schedule your paddle close to slack. Watch for some turbulence off major headlands along the south shore of Saturna.

Southerly winds can affect waters in Boundary Pass, whereas winds from the northwest affect waters in both the Strait of Georgia and Plumper Passage. Listen to wind predictions prior to paddling, paying particular attention to the reports for East Point.

This route is not for paddlers who are unfamiliar with calculating when it is safe to paddle through narrow passages. Given the likelihood of turbulent waters around East Point and the lack of suitable landings on the exposed southern shore of Saturna Island, this route is recommended for experienced paddlers only.

Getting There and Launching
The easiest launch for this route is from Saturna Island's Lyall Harbour government wharf. As the wharf is adjacent to the ferry terminal this option provides paddlers with the

opportunity of walking kayaks and gear onto Saturna–bound ferries. Immediately after unloading from the ferry, foot passengers turn left to access the government wharf. Those with vehicles turn right into the parking area in front of the general store, and wait until remaining ferry traffic passes. (Consider stocking up on last minute provisions.) Once the ferry has departed unload your gear and carry it down the ramp to the floating pier. Leave vehicles in a designated forty–eight–hour parking area about 200 m (650 ft) up from the ferry terminal. On a busy summer weekend, you may have to walk a fair distance back to the wharf.

The second launch is at the head of Lyall Harbour. Drive from the ferry terminal up the Narvaez Bay Road to the intersection with East Point Road. Turn left. At the bottom of the hill (about 1 km) turn left onto Sunset Boulevard. Launch from the bottom of the road. There are no signs indicating that you cannot park in this area.

The third launch provides quick access to the south side of Saturna. From the ferry terminal travel up Narvaez Bay Road to its intersection with East Point Road. Carry on a little further and make a right turn onto Harris Road. Travel down Harris past Money Lake and the Saturna Island Vineyards to Quarry Road. At the bottom of Quarry Road is Thomson Community Park. Launch from the sandy shore. Although there are no signs that indicate no overnight parking leave a note on the dash of your car indicating when you plan to return.

The fourth launch provides access to East Point and the south shore of Saturna. Drive from the ferry terminal up Narvaez Bay Road to the intersection with East Point Road. Turn left onto East Point Road and follow it all the way around to East Point Regional Park. (East Point Road becomes Tumbo Channel Road a few kilometers from the park.) There is a trail outside the park gate that provides beach access. It is a bit of hike down to the water with kayaks and gear but can be easily managed with cooperation between paddlers. Overnight parking is not permitted in the small parking lot at the head of the trail.

The Route

Although this route is described as a complete circumnavigation of Saturna paddlers may choose to do only one of two sections described: Lyall Harbour to Tumbo Island and East Point to Lyall Harbour. The launches for Saturna support paddling this route in its entirety or in sections.

Lyall Harbour to Tumbo Island

Cross the 0.5 nmi entrance to Lyall Harbour, heading toward the King Islets where shell beaches on the smaller of the two islets are particularly inviting. Minx Reef marks the entrance to Winter Cove, and although the shallows here pose little threat to shallow–draft boats, lookout for partially submerged, barnacle–covered rocks.

Located in the tiny cove along the south shore of Winter Cove is St. Christopher's Church. The rebuilt structure, originally a Japanese boathouse, once seated about twenty parishioners. It is no longer used.

St. Christopher's Church on the shore of Winter Cove. Photo: Bob Bruce.

The park in the northeast corner of Winter Cove serves well as a stopover while waiting for slack water in Boat Passage. This area was originally the site of an aggregates plant; the open pit quarry and furnace produced chipped stones for road building. Upon purchasing the land in 1979, the province established Winter Cove Marine Park. It is now part of the Gulf Islands National Park Reserve. There is currently no overnight camping here. However don't miss hiking the midden–lined trail to Winter Point. From the point, look out over Boat Passage, a dramatic portal between Saturna and Samuel Island—only 15 m (50 ft) wide! Water rushes into Winter Cove on the ebb in streams of up to 7 knots and on the flood spills into the strait. Apparently the hand pump in the picnic area is subject to contamination and subsequently closed for treatment. If you do need to top up your supply consider boiling water obtained here for a good ten minutes.

Swift tidal action in Boat Passage creates favourable fishing conditions for the river otter. On one occasion I watched four of these creatures. Every two minutes they would return to the surface with a small fish—their constant chatter proclaiming the success of their almost playful efforts. But swift currents create conditions that are not nearly as favourable for the paddler. Enter Boat Passage close to slack only; otherwise expect a vigorous 7–knot ride through the turbulent water.

Once through the pass, either cross over to the Belle Chain Group (see trip 12 for a description of the Belle Chain Islets) or head along Saturna's eastern shore toward Cabbage Island. Since this 4.5 mi stretch is open to northerly winds, check wind conditions for the Strait of Georgia prior to paddling.

Sloping sandstone shelves provide little in the way of stopovers on this side of Saturna. The few sandy shores are in front of private residences. The approach to Cabbage is studded with tiny islets, a favourite haul–out for seals. Pine Islet, the largest in the islet chain, joins Cabbage at low tide. In spring it is not uncommon to see hundreds of surf scooters here.

Cabbage Island

Camp locations on Cabbage Island—part of Gulf Islands National Park Reserve—are not only beautiful but are also easy to access. Land anywhere along the alluring white–sand beach on the island's south side. Forest–sheltered areas close to the sandy shore provide designated campsites. Pit toilets, a self–registration vault and information shelters are among the park's facilities. Consider swimming in the warm, aquamarine waters of Reef Harbour, or hike out along the shore for spectacular views out over the Strait of Georgia and distant mainland peaks. The widespread browning of trees in the middle of the island is the result of the effect of salt water. In the winter of 1982, high tides coupled with strong easterlies forced ocean water well above the high tide line, saturating the forest floor with salt.

After dark walk the waters edge and stir the nearby waters. Do the rippled waters give off tiny pinpricks of light? If so you are observing a rather unusual phenomenon called bioluminescence.

Bioluminescence

After dark, paddlers will notice that upon disturbing ocean water tiny pinpricks of light are observed, a rather unusual phenomenon called bioluminescence. Seawater is rich with tiny plankton that experience a population explosion during the summer (encouraged by warm water and increased sunlight). One particular species, *Noctiluca* (meaning "night light"), has a remarkable luminescence.

Noctiluca contains an enzyme, *luciferase*, and an organic compound, luciferin. When disturbed, the enzyme initiates a chemical reaction between luciferin and oxygen, and a pulse of light energy results. The movement of a paddle through the water, or feet through the sand, shifts the plankton, putting it in contact with the required oxygen. None of the energy released occurs as heat, the reference to "cold light." This phenomenon is best observed on a moonless night in the late summer.

Tumbo Island

Nearby Tumbo Island appears most inviting from any number of directions. Up until recently it was privately owned. Now its entire 121 hectares (300 acres) are within the Gulf Islands National Park Reserve and come under Parks Canada's jurisdiction. At the time of this writing (2003) Parks Canada planned to manage Tumbo for low impact recreational day–usage only. This may change on completion of the Park's final management plan. In the meantime paddlers will continue to camp on nearby Cabbage.

Campsite on Cabbage Island at low tide.
Photo: Andrew Madding.

First settled in 1877 several historic features on Tumbo provide evidence of past mining and fox farming. It is well worthwhile to hike the well marked trails. Either of the two obvious bays provides suitable landings. The bay facing toward Cabbage is very shallow. At high tide the upper beach makes for a suitable landing however low tide will present a muddy trek to paddlers. The east facing bay, nestled between Savage and Tumbo Point, provides the best landing and is by far the most alluring. Views from this shore across Boundary Pass to the American San Juans are fantastic. Be sure to pull your kayaks up high as this shoreline is subject to waves generated by passing freighters.

From either of these landings hike the perimeter of the wetlands. The unmistakable gurgle of red–wing blackbirds will mark your passage. Wander through Garry oaks, an old orchard and the once active farm. Look for evidence of past mining in the southern corner of the east facing bay. Don't miss hiking the sandstone shoreline out to Tumbo Point. From the point walk back along the obvious south shore trail through impressive Garry oak and arbutus forests. In the spring look for calypso orchids, western coral root, orange paintbrush, purple camas and at any time of year scan the treetops for eagle nesting sites.

~

Before you leave the sheltered waters around Cabbage and Tumbo give consideration to tide flows and the weather. Appropriately named Boiling Reef off the eastern tip of Saturna gives just cause for concern as turbulent waters reaching rates of up to 5 knots extend out from East Point in the form of huge whirls and eddylines all the way across to Tumbo Island. Schedule your paddling in the area close to slack. Using the Tide and Current Tables, slack is determined using the secondary station, Boundary Pass, on the reference, Race Passage. To get to East Point from Tumbo Island, paddle one of three options. The first follows the outer shoreline of Tumbo Island and, unless paddled close to slack, will likely require passing through the most extensive sections of turbulent water. The second follows the inner shores of Tumbo Island, riding the current in Tumbo Channel. (The current in this channel always flows in an easterly direction, a phenomenon that for paddlers heading from Cabbage to East Point works in their favour.) The sandstone cliffs on this side of Tumbo, although not high, are impressive. This second route will, however, require passing through some turbulent water, unless you are going through at slack. The third option avoids much of the East Point turbulence by angling across to Saturna Island before entering Tumbo Channel. Follow Saturna's shoreline closely, and round East Point by taking advantage of backeddies.

East Point to Lyall Harbour

Most paddlers presume that once they are around East Point, the effect of currents is minimal. Such is not the case. Maximum floods and ebbs create currents of up to 2 knots all the way from East Point to Taylor Point where currents are especially noticeable off major headlands. Take advantage of flows by making sure paddling direction and current direction are the same. On one occasion, I paddled against the current on the 1.5 mi stretch from Monarch Head to Taylor Point. It took forty–five minutes to cover the distance. On another trip, paddling

Sandstone cliffs along Saturna's southern shore. Photo: Tania Strauss.

Orca Whales

In 1964 a sculptor was commissioned by to go out and shoot a killer whale and then sculpt a life–size model for the Vancouver's new aquarium. A harpoon gun was set up on the southern shores of Saturna Island, and after a two–month vigil, a pod of thirteen approached the island shore. The harpoon was fired, injuring a youngster, but the orca did not die. Aquarium staff decided to move the one ton whale to Vancouver Harbour where over the next few weeks researchers fought desperately to save the life of the first–ever captive killer whale—Moby Doll. She, who actually turned out to be a he, didn't make it, but Moby's death brought world attention to a little–understood whale species, the orca whale.

Over the next decade the success of this capture sadly led to a lucrative live–captive fishery, with the orca of BC supplying aquariums around the world. Sixty–two were taken between 1965 and 1977. The impact this had on local populations caused concern to the public and to the many researchers anxious to find out more about the orca. By the late 70's this fishery was stopped and scientists began to study the occurrence and natural history of these magnificent whales. Over time each whale was identified by natural markings found on the dorsal fin and lighter–coloured saddle patches found at the base of the fin. Today, every resident orca on the BC coast has been identified and numbered.

Orcas are divided into three distinct communities—two are "resident," while a third is called "transient." One resident community, about 200 whales, is found off northern Vancouver Island and in Johnston Strait. The other resident community is found off southern Vancouver Island and is comprised of 3 smaller pods—J, K and L, with about eighty whales in all. J and K pods are the two most likely seen by paddlers visiting the Gulf Islands, whereas L pod is mostly seen along the southwest coast of Vancouver Island.

The transient community travels throughout the resident ranges. Over thirty transient pods have been recorded in these waters, but appear infrequently and at irregular times of the year. Their numbers are estimated at between 250 and 300 individuals. They do not mingle at all with residents.

The orca spend a good deal of time foraging, the residents feeding almost entirely on fish while transients prefer marine mammals such as porpoise and seals and, very infrequently, sea lions.

The resident population around southern Vancouver Island reached a high of 99 individuals in 1995. The numbers decreased to 79 individuals in 2001 and although numbers are again on the rise the overall decline has caused enough concern to declare this resident group endangered. Toxins that accumulate in top predators such as the orca whale may in part explain the decline. For the past 17 years Washington State's Centre for Whale Research, has focused on researching and tracking these resident pods. Check out their website at www.whaleresearch.com for recent updates on J, K and L pods. (The site even announces births and deaths.) Another site to check out is www.orcanetwork.org.. Consider supporting organizations such as these. They serve us well—on both sides of the border—by watching, recording and subsequently influencing, as best they can, any decision–making that could impact the future of the orca whale in these waters.

A fortunate paddler captures a shot of a surfacing orca whale. Photo: Maurice Robinson.

the same distance and riding a flooding current took only twenty minutes. One final note regarding currents in the area—unpredictable back– eddies, especially around Narvaez Bay, send currents flowing in the opposite direction from what is expected.

Boundary Pass is a huge body of water separating Canada and the United States. Freighters the size of city blocks use the pass as their gateway to the Strait of Georgia. Unless you are crossing over to the San Juans, their presence has little effect. But the winds that blow up Boundary Pass are a concern for paddlers. Listen to weather predictions, and if strong winds from the south are predicted, assume that they will affect paddling along this southeastern Saturna shore.

So, you have determined when to paddle around East Point, you know that you are paddling with current flows in Boundary Pass and weather

forecasts are predicting calm winds. Is this paddle worth all the scheduling required? You bet! The south shore of Saturna is magnificent. Immediately upon rounding East Point, you will see huge wave–sculpted sandstone cliffs rising 30 m (100 ft) or more to arbutus–covered ledges. Notice the many different ways the few residents here access the water from their homes—30 m above sea level! Ladders, ropes and railings of various lengths and degrees of maintenance dangle along the cliff face.

Fiddler's Cove

Don't miss a stopover in Fiddler's Cove. This is reserve land and is therefore private property. The Tsawout Band asks that you obtain permission to land or camp Obtain permission to camp by contacting the band manger. (For more information see "Reserve Lands" in the introduction.) Not only does the Tsawout Band typically permit exploring ashore here, but band members have generously granted the use of Fiddler's Cove for overnight camping. They ask that this privilege not be abused in any way, that fires are not lit and that all that is packed in is also packed out.

The cove's long sand beach is divided by a tiny islet that joins to the beach at low tide. Look for a trail leading away from the beach in the middle of the cove. It winds up the steep bank, traverses the top of nearby bluffs and eventually joins Fiddler's Road, a little–used offshoot of Saturna's East Point Road. Views from the top of the bluffs to the distant San Juans are worth the effort.

Narvaez Bay

Up until recently Narvaez Bay provided little in the way of a stopover for kayakers. However with the formation of the National Park Reserve in the Gulf Islands that has changed. Over 250 hectares (600 acres) of the steep forested shoreline on the southeast side of the bay are within the park. Land on either of the two pocket beaches, obvious on the chart, located on the point of land on the southeast corner of Narvaez Bay. Walk through old farmland, reputedly the first settlement on Saturna, linking one beach to the other. Although once logged the rich Douglas fir forest gives the impression that this area was undisturbed. Enjoy the quiet from the parks established picnic site above the inner of the two beaches. Previous undesignated camp areas such as this one will be reviewed by Parks Canada. An initial review should be completed during 2004. The review, which will take into account input from paddlers, may result in a designated campsite here – only however after careful consideration of potential impacts.

~

The cliffs between Narvaez Bay and Monarch Head are undoubtedly the most magnificent on Saturna's shores. Their 60 m (200 ft) rise significantly dwarfs paddlers below. Falcons and eagles ride the thermals above the highest ledges.

Two coves just inside Monarch Head are accessible only at high tide as at low tide huge boulders block access to the sand beaches above. Those fortunate enough to land can walk through the open arbutus forest to the point. I watched as a pod of orca passed this point during an unforgettable lunch stop. It is common to view resident orca in Boundary Pass.

Paddle close to the rocky shoreline between Monarch Head and Bruce Bight, and look into the clear waters for white plumose anemones, red and purple urchins and ochre stars. Here, seals often pull out on exposed rock ledges, raccoons scour the intertidal zone for molluscs and overhead eagles scan the water for prey.

Paddling the pass between Java Islets and Saturna's shore against current flows will noticeably deter progress. Paddle through with the current or close to slack.

Remains of the old stone house at Taylor Bay. Photo: Andrew Madding.

Taylor Bay

Sheltered by Taylor Point is a magnificent sand beach and a meadow owned for years by longtime Saturna residents, the Campbells. The 4 km stretch from Taylor Bay beach around to Trueworthy Bight is now included in the Gulf Islands National Park Reserve. A trail will be developed along this stretch by Parks Canada over the next few years. Watch for trailhead signs once it is in place. In the meantime explore the meadow above the beach and the remains of the old stone house. Don't miss a walk around the outside of Taylor Point, originally owned by George Taylor, who at the turn of the century operated a stone quarry, as evidenced by the angular cuts in the rock. Apparently, some of the stone was used in the construction of the Parliament Buildings in

Victoria. Underwater divers visiting Taylor Point take delight in the numerous bottles and other pieces of debris that were dumped from the wharf long ago. Management plans for this section of the park are focused on conservation. Recreational opportunities are, for now, restricted to low impact day use activities.

~

Kayak landings from Taylor Point to Crocker Point are made difficult by barnacle–covered rock ledges. Yes, a murder did actually occur at Murder Point. An American and his daughter were killed here by natives in the winter of 1863. The story tells of an entire family moving from Waldron Island (US) to Mayne Island in a small boat. When a storm hit, most of the family were transported by a local, while the father and one daughter stayed behind with their possessions. They were attacked by a group of Lamalchi Indians. No one knows exactly why these supposedly innocent victims were murdered; it could be that another completely unconnected incident may have prompted the attack. Eleven natives were implicated, three of whom were convicted of murder and eventually hanged in Victoria.

Once around the point, paddlers may feel the effect of an ebb tide flowing out of Plumper Sound, although flows seldom exceed 1 knot. Winds from the north and northwest have more of an effect on paddling when winds from the Strait of Georgia spill into Plumper Sound.

At 490 m (1630 ft) Mount Warburton Pike is a striking landmark. The mountain is named after a unique Oxford graduate, who arrived here in the 1880s and is best remembered for his eccentric and colourful personality. Warburton Pike would apparently disappear for months on end, wear tailored suits until they fell off his back and go barefoot so often that he could use his toes as if they were fingers. Rated as one of the top big–game hunters in the world, he acquired a reputation as an explorer after making two great journeys into the Canadian north (Wolferstan). Pike bought the farm at the foot of the mountain that eventually bore his name. Today, Mount Warburton Pike, along with Mount Fischer, Mount David, Winter Cove and Narvaez Bay forms the largest single protected area in the Gulf Islands National Park Reserve. A rare stand of virgin Douglas fir at the summit was protected initially with Ecological Reserve and now with National Park Reserve status.

Paddle around Crocker Point into Breezy Bay. Breezy Bay's Saturna Beach was the site of the island's famous Dominion Day Lamb Barbecue. The event that started in 1950 as a school picnic grew so much that, in the 1980s, crowds of two thousand came to join the festivities. In 1989, the fortieth anniversary of the event, the festivities moved to Winter Cove. Today, this beach and the surrounding area form a regional community park called Thomson Park. The small wharf is public. The adjacent larger wharf is owned by Saturna Island Vineyards providing visitors a convenient landing and access to local wine tasting.

Elliot Bluff rises 30 m (100 ft) or more above sea level, providing high–rise–style accommodation for resident cormorants. Boot Cove is worth exploring if there is time but provides little in the way of beach exploration as most of the shoreline is inhabited. What is most interesting about this cove is a deceptive calm, for although it appears to be sheltered, in fact it is not. Apparently, winds are funneled by the cove's steep sides, and speeds up to 130 km per hour (80 mph) have been recorded. Paddlers can take comfort in knowing that the funneling occurs during winter months, less so in the spring and autumn and not at all in the summer.

Paddle back to Lyall Harbour to spend a ferry–wait on the balcony of the Lighthouse Pub, overlooking Plumper Sound.

11 Saturna to South Pender

Difficulty Intermediate conditions – moderate risk
Distance 13 nmi
Duration 2 days
Charts 3441 – Haro Strait, Boundary Pass and Satellite Channel (1:40,000)
Tides Reference Port: Fulford Harbour
Secondary Port: Bedwell Harbour
Currents Reference Station: Race Passage
Secondary Station: Boundary Passage
Camping South Pender Island – Beaumont Park
Land Jurisdictions Gulf Islands National Park Reserve – Beaumont /Mount Norman Park and Blunden Islet

Archaeological excavations on the Pender Canal revealed that native peoples inhabited these shores for at least five thousand years. View these impressive midden sites, then paddle along forested Bedwell Harbour to Beaumont Park. Access an extensive network of park trails, then camp under an evergreen canopy. Paddle Pender's outer shores, watching for the pods of orca that frequently visit these waters.

Paddling Considerations
Currents in Plumper Sound are minimal, and during the summer, winds are often calm to light. However, Plumper Sound is open to winds from northern quadrants. Strong north winds that blow down the Strait of Georgia spill into these waters. The shores of South Pender are exposed to winds from the south. Listen to wind predictions for the general area, paying particular attention to predictions for the strait.

Watch for turbulence off major headlands along the south shore of South Pender, especially around Blunden Islet.

Given the 1.5 mi crossing from Saturna to the Penders and the exposure to winds, this route is not recommended for novice paddlers.

Getting There and Launching
The launches for this route are the same as those for trip 10, Saturna Island. Refer to the Lyall Harbour and Thomson Community Park launch for the Saturna paddle.

The Route
Paddle this route separately or as an extension of the Saturna route. It is written here assuming a launch from the Lyall Harbour wharf.

From Lyall Harbour, head west toward Elliot Bluff, leaving the bluffs at their midpoint and navigating toward Pender's Razor Point. The Plumper Sound crossing is 1.5 nmi.

Arbutus–studded Razor Point marks the entrance to Port Browning, at the head of which is a waterside pub serving not only brew, but also pub–style meals.

Some paddlers may elect to miss Port Browning and paddle directly

Beach fronting the campsites on Bedwell Harbour. Photo: Andrew Madding.

from Razor Point to Mortimer Spit, a narrow band of sand and shells forming one side of Shark Cove. A gently sloped beach is excellent for landing kayaks or canoes. The numerous holes visible in the sand at low tide indicate that there is a large clam population here.

One more stop must be made before entering the Pender Canal. Head to the gravel bar right of the bridge. (Pull kayaks well up on shore as pleasure boats frequently use the canal and create a fair bit of swell.) The bank immediately above the beach is comprised of shells deposited over several millennia, creating an impressive shell midden. Archaeological excavations have produced evidence of native occupation going back five thousand years. A second midden site, equally as significant, is accessed by crossing the road

and following the short trail from the right side of the bridge. These lands are owned by the province and protected by heritage conservation laws.

Now back to the Pender Canal. At one time, North and South Pender were joined by a narrow spit, and a portage was necessary to avoid rowing all the way around the island. The canal that created the two Penders was excavated in 1903. The bridge reuniting North and South Pender was not built until 1955. Flows in the canal reach 3 knots, with currents strongest around the bridge pilings. If you get beyond them, assume passage will be easier through the remainder of the channel. Listen for the rattle call of the kingfisher here. The cutaway banks on the South Pender side of the canal are prime nest–building habitat for these crested birds.

Paddle the north side of Bedwell Harbour to Ainslie Point and a delightful pocket–shaped beach tucked inside the point. Head on to Bedwell Harbour. The combined 160 hectares (400 acres) of the former provincial Beaumont Marine Park and regional Mount Norman Park have been transferred to the new the National Park Reserve. Together they form a significant protected area on Pender Island. During the summer this area is very busy with boat traffic. There is a marina and a Canada Customs checkpoint nearby along with several mooring buoys. Paddlers who prefer more seclusion will likely choose to pass by. Others may consider an overnight stop in the spring and fall or even during peak summer months with awareness that campsites are little used as most yachtspeople return to their boats at sundown.

Look closely at the grassy isthmus that links the small rock peninsula to the mainland—it is made up of shell midden. Scattered throughout the adjacent woodlands are 11 walk–in campsites and a pump that yields water all summer! The self–registration vault accepts the nominal camping fee.

Spend some time exercising the lower limbs by hiking up the 244–m (800 ft) high Mount Norman. As you climb, arbutus–covered bluffs give way to thick Douglas fir and red cedar forests. Logging, which has intermittently occurred over the past several decades, is in evidence about halfway up. Within an hour you will reach the top to take in your just reward—a magnificent view of the San Juans and distant Gulf Islands.

East of Beaumont Park is Poets Cove Resort, a rather posh establishment offering moorage and marina facilities, likely of little interest to paddlers except for a store, showers and waterside pub.

At this point, inexperienced paddlers may choose to retrace the described route back to Saturna, thereby avoiding a paddle around the south end of Pender.

The outer coast of South Pender is exposed to south winds, and currents are noticeable off major headlands, especially off Teece Point and Blunden Islet during peak floods and ebbs. A large number of homes line these shores, and although beaches suitable for landing are frequent, most are adjacent to private residences. In the event of an emergency land just inside and east of Tilly Point.

Blunden Islet is protected with National Park Reserve status. This islet shows little or no evidence of invasion by exotic species thereby providing an excellent example of coastal bluff vegetation. Steep rocky shorelines discourage any landings on Blunden.

From Teece Point, return to Saturna, navigating toward the open slopes of Mount Warburton Pike. Wind patterns in this part of the world can be unpredictable. It is common to round Teece Point on a seemingly calm day only to encounter a north wind blowing down Plumper Sound. About two–thirds of the way across the sound and closer to Saturna, southerly winds can have the greater influence. Summer wind strengths are usually manageable, but listen to wind predictions prior to making this 1.5 nmi crossing.

5,000 Years on the Pender Canal

Interest in excavating the Pender Canal site was first expressed by archaeologists in the 1960s as severe erosion was destroying the significant midden. But the owners of the property were reticent to agree to excavations. The site was finally purchased by the province, and when various proposals to halt the erosion proved impractical, a decision to excavate was made.

Archaeologists from Simon Fraser University coordinated excavations here in the mid 1980s. The site, completely cleared of underbrush and gridded in 2 m (6 ft) squares, was meticulously excavated 10 cm (4 in) at a time. All artifacts were recorded, mapped, numbered and analyzed—a huge project considering that thousands of archaeological features were discovered. The tiniest bone fragments and bits of flaked stone were all treated as important objects within the assemblage. Slate knives, rock adzes, basalt abraders, bone awls and antler wedges are only a few of the prehistoric tools uncovered. Perhaps most exciting are the burials, some completely intact, others mere scattered remains. A slate box received the most attention. Simply constructed of stone, the cover and four slab walls likely functioned as a storage container.

Although most of the artifacts are dated 2500 to 4000 years old, some are as old as 5,000 years.

12 Belle Chain Islets, South Mayne and Samuel Island

Difficulty Intermediate conditions – moderate risk
Distance 7 nmi round trip
Duration Day trip
Charts 3441 – Haro Strait, Boundary Pass and Satellite Channel (1:40,000)
Tides Reference Ports: Fulford Harbour and Point Atkinson
  Secondary Ports: Samuel Island, South Shore and Samuel Island, North Shore
Current Reference Station: Active Pass
  Secondary Stations: Boat Passage and Georgeson Passage
Camping No camping
Land Jurisdictions Gulf Islands National Park Reserve – Belle Chain Islets

The true highlight of this trip has to be the Belle Chain. Distant Coast Mountains are an impressive backdrop for this magnificent archipelago. California and Steller sea lions typically haul out on these tiny islets from fall to spring, masterfully commanding respect from all passers by, and year round, harbour seals swim in the surrounding kelp–choked shallows.

Paddling Considerations
Tidal streams reach up to 5 knots in Georgeson Passage and 7 knots in Boat Passage. Flows in both passages demand scheduling so that passing through them occurs close to slack.

During the summer, the winds in the Strait of Georgia that blow from the north demand consideration. Listen to wind predictions for the strait prior to paddling, and pay particular attention to the conditions described from the East Point Light Station.

Because of its exposure to winds in the Strait of Georgia, and because of strong currents in two of its passes, this route is for experienced paddlers.

Getting There and Launching

To access the two Mayne Island launches from either Tsawwassen or Swartz Bay ferry terminals board Village Bay–bound ferries. A fifteen–minute drive across Mayne Island is necessary to access the launch site. From the ferry terminal, follow Village Bay Road to the Fernhill Road junction where a general store supplies last minute provisions. A left turn leads to Springwater Lodge, Mayne Island's only pub. Here, you may sit out on the balcony overlooking Active Pass, sip a pint and enjoy some pub fare. Return to the intersection of Village Bay Road and Fernhill Road. Follow Fernhill until it becomes Bennett Bay Road. Follow Bennett Bay Road to Isabella Lane. Turn left onto Isabella then take the next right. Follow this short lane to its Bennett Bay terminus. Launch from the beach on Bennett Bay. The sandy expanse on Bennett Bay and out to Campbell Point is within the Gulf Islands National Park Reserve.

The second launch is accessed by continuing further along Bennett Bay Road until it becomes Arbutus Drive. Follow Arbutus Drive and within a short distance look to the right for Seaview Road. At the intersection with Seaview Road turn left onto an unnamed lane. A beach and an adjacent parking area located at the bottom of this lane provide easy water access.

The Route

This route can be paddled on its own as a day trip or as an extension of the Saturna route by launching from either Bennett Bay on Mayne Island or from Lyall Harbour on Saturna Island. The description here assumes a day trip and a launch from Bennett Bay.

Paddlers may find it difficult to leave the sandy shores on Bennett Bay. The 11 ha (27 acres) that surround the bay and extend out to Campbell Point were purchased by the Marine Heritage Legacy in 1996 and were transferred to the Gulf Islands National Park Reserve in 2003. If the lure of sun and sand is not too great depart from Bennett Bay. Navigate toward the two unnamed islets off the north side of Samuel Island, recognizing that once away from the protection offered by Georgeson Island, the route is exposed to potential northerly winds. Stay clear of the turbulence off Samuel Island's Granger Point, especially when flood waters from Georgeson Passage spill out into the Strait of Georgia. Both Georgeson Island and Georgeson Passage are named after a well–known Gulf Islands family. Two generations of Georgesons manned Saturna's East Point lighthouse for over fifty years. Georgeson Island has recently been included in the Gulf islands National Park Reserve. Occupied only seasonally for many years, this relatively intact island will be managed to preserve the old growth Douglas fir and Garry oak forests. Consider a short daytime stop–over to take in unob-

Looking across to Samuel Island from Saturna's Winter Cove. Photo: Andrew Madding.

structed views of Mount Baker and the nearby Belle Chain Islets.

In the previous version of Island Paddling I suggested heading to the two unnamed islets off Samuel's north shore. I also made reference to a couple of fairly obscure camp locations. In this version I discourage visiting either of these two islets. Landing on the sandstone ledges is difficult and these little–visited islets are best left unaltered. Take them in from the water's edge.

The highlight of this trip is the Belle Chain Islets. Recently included in the Gulf Island National Park Reserve, this rocky archipelago is made all the more magnificent with the snow–capped, coast mountain backdrop. Exposed ledges are a favourite haul–out for harbour seals.

But most impressive are the Steller and California sea lions that return here annually. Early arrivals appear in October and use the islets as a haul–out until the following spring, when they return to distant breeding grounds. Listen for their loud barks from the launch in Bennett Bay to be assured of their presence. For the closest view of these huge pinnipeds, determine current direction, then, from an upstream position, drift alongside the beached lions. Avoid paddling as flailing blades will alert them to your presence. A respectful distance is required—paddle too close and sea lions will plunge into the water and masterfully command your respect.

Anniversary Island, the largest islet in the Belle Chain group, provides an opportunity to land. Scout out the most level of the rock ledges on the east point, recognizing that even the best of landings will require some maneuvering over sloping sandstone. The grassy knoll immediately above the shore provides an alluring lunch stop. Watch eagles and cormorants attracted to a weather–worn snag, and listen to the whistle of pigeon guillemots as they fly out from their protective rock crevices. I am certain Parks Canada will give careful consideration to usage of this island. Although I suggested camping here in a previous edition of Island Paddling, in recognition of the sensitivity of this ecosystem, the increasing number of paddlers and the addition of parklands on Tumbo, I would now suggest limiting visits to daytime or setting up camp on nearby Cabbage.

At this point paddlers may choose to extend the route by heading east to Cabbage Island and linking up with trip 10, Saturna Island Circumnavigation. Otherwise, make the 0.5 mi crossing to the eastern tip of Samuel Island, entering Boat Passage, a dramatic 15 m (50 ft) opening between Samuel and Saturna Islands. The pass demands that paddlers schedule their passing through, as water gushes through the narrow gap at all but slack water. Passage at any time other than slack could be treacherous. Refer to the current reference for Boat Passage in the Tide and Current Tables. Further description of both Boat Passage and adjacent Winter Cove are provided in trip 10.

The south side of Samuel Island boasts several sandy beaches, most within Irish Bay. I have never landed at Samuel Island as an ever present caretaker conscientiously discourages anyone from stopping. The meadow, seen from both Winter Cove and Irish Bay, is the result of the hard labours of one of the original owners of the island, Archie Grey. In the 1930s and 1940s, E. P. Taylor bred and trained racehorses here until he sold the 132 ha (328 ac) island to Charles Lindbergh's daughter for $48,000.

Samuel Island has an interesting tide pattern. Tides on the south side of the island are calculated using Fulford Harbour as a reference port. Tides on the north side are reckoned using Point Atkinson, north of Vancouver on the Strait of Georgia, as a reference port. Range differences between the tide levels often exceed 0.5 m (1.6 ft), yet the two references are only metres apart.

On to Georgeson Passage. Forested shores flank both sides of this river–like pass. Tidal streams reach up to 4 knots—speeds that a paddler does not wish to be working against. Pass through at slack, or take advantage of a free ride on a gentle flood tide, and watch for eddylines in the shallows off Lizard and Curlew Islands and around the islets off Granger Point.

Plan a side trip into Horton Bay. The waters here, sheltered by Curlew, are often mirror–still. A picturesque farm nestled in the head of the bay enhances the pastoral appeal of this shoreline. Tie up to the government float, and wander up the roadway through lush woodlands.

Return to the launch following south shore of Bennett Bay.

5 Saltspring, Prevost and Galiano Islands

Those new to the sport of sea kayaking will find this area most appealing. The waters along these routes are largely sheltered from the prevailing winds. The open water stretches are short in distance and current action is minimal. Novice and experienced paddlers alike will discover the hours slipping by as they paddle past the quiet isolation of Prevost shores, naturally sculpted sandstone cliffs and a secluded saltwater lagoon. Easily accessed from any number of launch sites visitors to this area are sure to be lulled by a slower pace and a natural beauty.

Unpacking the boats. James bay, Prevost Island. Photo: Andrew Madding.

Ballingal Islets

Wise Island

Charles Island

Porlier Pass Road

Montague Harbour

Parker Island

Sturdies Bay Road

Galiano Island

Churchill Road launch

Trincomali Channel

Long Harbour Road

Active Pass

Long Harbour

Chain Islands

Wellbury Bay

Peile Point

James Bay

Village Bay

Mayne Island

Hawkins Islet

Ganges Harbour

Selby Point

Prevost Island

Portlock Point

Red Islets

North Pender Island

Saltspring

Island

Ackland Islets

Point Lidell

Swanson Channel

Otter Bay

N

launch	⬤
campsite	Λ
marina	M
ferry terminal	F

0   nmi   2

13 Saltspring's Long Harbour and Chain Islands

Difficulty Novice conditions – minimal risk
Distance 5 nmi – Long Harbour, 5 nmi – Chain Islands
Duration Day trip
Chart No. 3442, North Pender to Thetis Island (1 40,000)
Tides Reference Port: Fulford Harbour
Secondary Port: Ganges Harbour
Currents Not applicable
Camping No camping

How about a weekend getaway to the Gulf Islands? Stay at one of Saltspring's charming Bed and Breakfasts, and take along kayaks and gear in anticipation of some relaxed, short–distance paddling. Both Long Harbour and the Chain Group beg to be explored during a winter reprieve.

Paddle the mirror–still lagoon at the head of Long Harbour, and explore the nearby estuary, or take shelter in a cove behind the tiny islets that mark the entrance to the harbour. Head over to the Chain Group, a delightful archipelago that is not only beautiful but is also historically fascinating.

Paddling Considerations

Currents are minimal in both Ganges and Long Harbours. Winds are generally calm during the summer. However, both harbours are open to the occasional southeaster.

These routes are well suited to the novice paddler.

Getting There and Launching

Both Long Harbour and the Chain Islands routes are accessible to walk–on paddlers from the mainland, as ferries that leave Tsawwassen dock in Long

Harbour. Look for the Long Harbour launch on the Wellbury Bay side of the ferry terminal where an access trail leads from the parking area down to the water.

For paddlers arriving with vehicles drive onto a Long Harbour–bound ferry departing from Tsawwassen or a Fulford Harbour–bound ferry departing from Swartz Bay. Either way, head toward Saltspring Island's Ganges Harbour and the nearby Churchill Road launch site. (If you are driving from Ganges Harbour toward Long Harbour look to the right for Churchill Road. It is located within a couple of kilometres of Ganges.) At the end of Churchill Road is a public beach access. Park vehicles and hike the short trail down to Ganges Harbour. The banks along this trail reveal an impressive shell midden.

The Route

From the Long Harbour ferry terminal, paddle to the head of the inlet where docks, mooring buoys and private homes are plentiful. Beyond this development, the inlet narrows to a passageway leading to a secluded lagoon, where the already quiet waters are hushed further by

The Arbutus

The arbutus, or madrone, is Canada's only broadleafed evergreen. Specially adapted oval leaves are glossy on the upper side, allowing water to run off them easily. In the event of freezing temperatures, an icy coating does not develop on the leaves. The tree's most outstanding characteristics are its peeling green bark and its twisted, copper–coloured trunk. In March it blooms with clusters of creamy white flowers. In the fall the blossoms develop into small orange–red berries. The arbutus thrives on exposed rocky bluffs overlooking the sea throughout the Gulf Islands where even under the best conditions it rarely exceeds 12 m (40 ft).

the thick forest that surrounds these shores. At the end of the lagoon is a small estuary, and at high tide, deeper waters allow passage through to the marshy terminus.

Return to the main harbour, and follow its north shore to Nose Point. This entire stretch of coast is part of a development called "Maracaibo Estates." The homes are few and well hidden, as their natural wood finish blends in well with the forest environment. White–shell beaches are frequent along the route. Clamshell Island, in the middle of the harbour, calls out to be explored. However, steep rocky banks deter landing. Those disappointed by poor access may take comfort in knowing the island supports a prolific growth of prickly pear. Out toward Nose Point, thick rain forest gives way to open woodlands, and a small cove, sheltered from wind and view by a cluster of tiny islets, is worth exploring.

At this point paddlers may choose to link up with the Chain Islands or Prevost Island routes or simply return to the ferry terminal following Long Harbour's southern shore. There are many more homes on this side of Long Harbour. The most impressive complex serves as an outstation for the Royal Vancouver Yacht Club.

If paddling near the ferry terminal, be aware that because Long Harbour is so narrow, the ferries that arrive at least twice daily must go beyond the dock and then back up into the slip.

The Chain Islands

The Chain Islands in the middle of Ganges Harbour provide for an interesting shoreline paddle.

Recent history is in evidence on First Sister Island. Upon purchasing the island in the 1920s, an immigrant Scotsman decided he should live in a home reminiscent of his homeland, and so this rather colourful individual proceeded to construct a scaled–down version of an authentic Scottish castle. Alas, the unfortunate fellow was also fond of alcoholic beverage, and it eventually did him in. An American subsequently purchased the medieval real estate but soon discovered it was not only much too primitive, but that it was also impossible to heat! He had a large portion of it torn down. However, the remains of the original castle are visible on the island today.

A beautiful white–shell beach on the west end of Third Sister Island shouldn't be missed.

Several mammals inhabit these waters. Expect to see mink and river otter, and perhaps fallow deer. On a particular winter paddle, I sat and watched a deer swim to the most easterly islet of the Deadman Group. The young buck went ashore and proceeded to browse the undergrowth. Deer frequently swim across saltwater passages in the hopes of reaching better forage.

In the summer, Ganges Harbour becomes very busy, as it is a major thoroughfare for boat traffic. At the head of the harbour is the community of Ganges, one of the largest in the Gulf Islands, offering a variety of services and facilities. Grocery stores, bakeries, restaurants, craft stores and a liquor outlet may be of interest to paddlers—all within walking distance of the government wharves.

14 Prevost Island

Difficulty Beginner conditions – low risk
Distance 8 nmi – circumnavigation of Prevost
12 nmi – circumnavigation of Prevost and inlets
Duration 1 – 2 days
Chart 3442, North Pender to Thetis Island (1:40,000)
Tides Reference Port: Fulford Harbour
Secondary Ports: Ganges Harbour and Montague   Harbour
Currents Reference Station: Race Passage
Secondary Stations: Swanson Channel and Trincomali Channel
Camping Prevost Island – James Bay
Land Jurisdictions Gulf Islands National Park Reserve – James Bay, Hawkins, Bright and Red Islets, Richardson Bay

Since 1924 Prevost Island has been farmed by the DeBurgh family, and to this day the tended fields and rough pastures support domestic herds. The resulting pastoral countryside stands out in distinct contrast to the busier Gulf Islands.

A stunning piece of property surrounding the island's James Bay is now within the Gulf Islands National Park Reserve. An overnight visit to a delightful isle that has maintained its charm and quiet isolation is now possible.

Paddling Considerations
Currents are minimal. The only riffling of waters occurs off Selby Point (during peak tide flows only).

Winds are generally calm, and only when strong winds blow from the southern quadrants do the waves increase to a significant height.

This trip is well suited to beginner paddlers.

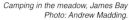
Camping in the meadow, James Bay
Photo: Andrew Madding.

Getting There and Launching

The most accessible launch for Prevost Island is Saltspring Island's Churchill Road access. It is described in detail for trip 13, Saltspring's Long Harbour and Chain Islands. The distance from this launch to Prevost Island's Selby Point is about 3.5 nmi.

Prevost is also accessible by launching at Otter Bay Marina on Pender Island. Otter Bay is within 0.5 km (0.3 mi) of Pender's ferry slip. Paddlers may either walk wheeled kayaks to this launch site or drive to it. Look to the right for the marina turn-off within a couple of hundred metres of leaving the ferry terminal. The marina deservedly charges a minimal launch fee.

Three other launches for Prevost are adjacent to ferry terminals on Mayne, Pender and Saltspring Islands, making it possible to leave vehicles at Tsawwassen and Swartz Bay terminals. However, be aware that these launches are not as easily accessed. Two of the three launches also require crossing ferry–infested Swanson Channel. Ferries run so frequently in the summer it is difficult to time an anxiety–free crossing.

The first launch is adjacent to Saltspring's Long Harbour ferry terminal. A detailed description of this launch is provided in the launch section for trip 13, Long Harbour and Chain Islands. The paddling distance from this launch to Prevost Island is 2 nmi. Ferries are not a concern on this crossing.

The second launch is accessed immediately to the right of Pender Island's ferry slip. However, negotiating kayaks and gear past a thriving take–out business and over large blocks of concrete makes this launch tricky. Paddling distance to Prevost is about 2 nmi. Watch out for ferries.

The third launch is close to Mayne Island's ferry terminal. Immediately upon leaving the ferry, look for a gate in the terminal's fencing and a short trail that leads to a sandy–shore launch. Paddling distance to Prevost is 1.5 nmi. Be aware, however, that this crossing is also an extraordinary time–management exercise as paddlers attempt to dodge ferries that frequently enter and exit Active Pass.

Prevost could also be easily accessed by those paddling in the Sidney area. (Refer to trip 9, Portland, Moresby and Russell Islands.) From Portland Island, cross to Russell

The Sea Urchin

What is most remarkable about the urchin is a complex chewing mechanism composed of forty bones and sixty muscles. It is called "Aristotle's Lantern" since it reminded the scientist/philosopher Aristotle of a many–sided lantern. Located on its underside, this mouth scrapes and tears plant material from the sea floor, quickly changing an expansive garden of kelp into a pavement of pink cructose algae.

Understandably, the spiny urchin has few predators, so juveniles settle close to the adults where they are protected under the canopy of spines.

Urchins are commercially fished in BC waters to meet the demands of an inexhaustible Japanese market. The roe, extracted from the urchin and placed in shallow trays for export, is consumed raw and must therefore arrive fresh and in prime condition.

Exploring ashore on the Hawkins Islets. Photo: Kelly Irving.

Island then Ruckle Park on the southeast corner of Saltspring. Cross Captain Passage to the Channel Islands (the Channel Islands are within the Gulf Islands National Park Reserve) and then head to Prevost, a total distance of about 5 nmi.

Prevost is also accessible to those paddling Galiano routes (trip 15, Galaino Island – Montague Harbour). The distance from Galiano's Montague Harbour to Prevost is about 3 nmi. Ferries are not a concern on this Trincomali Channel crossing.

The Route

The route described here assumes a launch from Saltspring Island's Churchill Road access. Paddle the northern shore of Ganges Harbour heading toward Scott Point. (See trip 13, the Chain Islands section, for a description.) From Scott Point cross over to Nose Point, then begin a 0.5–mi crossing over to Prevost's Selby Point. Captain Passage narrows here, and as a result, currents can pick up speed. However, it is easy to get around Selby Point, even when paddling against flows.

Up until recently paddlers did not have other than below high tide line access to Prevost shores. However, in the mid 90s, 125 ha (340 ac) of land surrounding James Bay (including the entire Peile Point peninsula) were purchased by the provincial and federal governments and in 2004 these lands were transferred to the Gulf islands National Park Reserve. Parks Canada intends to maintain the primitive camping usage historically accessed from the head of the bay. O'Reilly Beach is the local name given to this cove where the large meadow and orchard add to it's pastoral appeal. There is plenty of opportunity for on–foot exploration nearby. Wander inland through open fields and forest trails. Or simply explore the shoreline around the bay. The more intrepid paddler may choose to hike the 1 km (.6 mi) trail out to Peile Point.

Paddle Around Provost Island

Weekend visitors will discover it fairly easy to depart from James Bay Saturday morning to paddle Prevost's 7.5 km circumference and return to camp by Saturday evening.

Paddle from Peile to Portlock Point. Although the rocky shoreline and thick forest growing right down to the water don't provide land access along this stretch of coast, the views to the rock bluffs on Galiano and down to Active Pass are magnificent. In the spring herring attract hundreds of migratory birds to this area, including oldsquaws, scooters and Brandt's cormorants.

The Hawkins Islets, also included in the National Park Reserve, are well worth a close–to–shore exploration. Low tides expose nearby reefs where harbour seals bask in the sun. Magnificent displays of the red sea urchin are visible in the shadows off the south islet. In spring, the wildflowers that cover these islets create a vivid palate of colour. Chocolate lilies, pink sea–blush, yellow buttercups, blue camas, white saxifrage and blue–eyed Mary all bloom simultaneously. Pad-

Paddling off Portlock point, Prevost Island. Photo: Kelly Irving.

dlers may be tempted to go ashore however access is very limited. Years ago I camped solo on the islet but was perched somewhat precariously on the little available level land. Leave ecologically fragile Hawkins to viewing from water level.

The little lighthouse on Portlock Point, built in 1896, was manned up until 1969. One of the keepers died in a fire that destroyed the keepers house in 1964. Portlock's light heralds an attractive shell beach in Richardson Bay. This sheltered gem will lure many a paddler ashore as the beach and adjacent 25 ha (62 acre) forest are all within the Gulf islands National Park Reserve. Before you explore ashore place kayaks high enough to avoid ferry–generated swell from dumping into open cockpits.

Groves of arbutus and Garry oaks, drying reefs off the Bright Islets, ferries passing and views down Swanson Channel all add to the spectacular stretch of coast from Portlock Point to the Red Islets. The beautiful Red Islets are also within the national park. In the previous version of this guide I suggested camping there. However with the creation of new parklands on Prevost's James Bay and Richardson Bay I would suggest leaving these relatively intact, environmentally sensitive islets to a short stopover or viewing from the water. Paddlers can land on either of two white–shell beaches on the outer tip of the largest islet. At high water, access is straightforward, but at low water, it is necessary to carry kayaks over exposed rocks.

Arbutus trees cling tenaciously to the tops of the rock bluffs from Point Lidell to Glenthorne Passage. Offshore, the Ackland Islands jut abruptly from sea level to a crown of evergreen. The island's close proximity to Prevost creates a delightful passage, where seals observe passing paddlers.

Secret Island is no secret. Cabins front onto both Captain and Glenthorne Passages. Glenthorne Passage is no secret either. On a summer day, many boaters seek shelter here and for good reason—it is exceptionally beautiful. To fully appreciate this specific area's charm, plan a visit in the spring or fall.

Paddle along the Glenthorne Passage shoreline to where the isthmus between Glenthorne and Annette Inlet reaches its narrowest point. The banks are speckled white with shells that form a large midden. The dock visible at the head of Glenthorne Passage is the main access to the farm on Prevost.

Annette Inlet is the longest inlet indenting Prevost, about 1 nmi in length. Several shell middens found along the bank indicate that native people frequently visited these shores. Herons commonly fish the shallows at the head of the inlet.

Don't miss Selby Cove. Steep overhanging cliffs on the western shore are lush with the green of ferns and forest. A meadow at the head of the inlet enhances the pastoral landscape. Park land fronts a section of the eastern shore. Steep slopes, however, make access to the park from this vantage impractical.

Either return to camp in James Bay or to Saltspring's Churchill Road launch.

15 Galiano Island – Montague Harbour

Difficulty Beginner conditions – low risk
Distance 7 nmi round trip
Duration Day trip
Chart 3442, North Pender to Thetis Island (1:40,000)
Tides Reference Port: Fulford Harbour
Secondary Port: Montague Harbour
Currents Reference Station: Race Passage
Secondary Station: Trincomali Channel
Camping Montague Harbour Park
Land Jurisdictions Gulf Island National Park Reserve – Montague Harbour

Some paddlers may choose to avoid this area during the busier summer months, but paddled in the off–season, this route is special. Particularly noteworthy are the hundreds of migratory birds that return annually to these waters. Remarkable at any time of the year are the naturally sculpted sandstone cliffs on the shores of Galiano.

Paddling Considerations

For the most part, currents in this area are minimal, seldom exceeding 1.5 knots. (Paddlers may wish to coordinate a northward paddle with a flood tide and a southward paddle with the ebb.) The stronger currents swirling around the tiny islets off the west end of Parker Island are usually manageable and easily avoided. Winds here are generally calm, but watch for occasional southerlies that blow up Trincomali Channel.

The likelihood of favourable paddling conditions makes this a suitable route for beginner paddlers.

Getting There and Launching

To access the Galiano Island launch, board ferries bound for the island at either the Swartz Bay or Tsawwassen terminal. From Galiano Island's Sturdies Bay terminal, follow Sturdies Bay Road to Georgeson Bay Road. Turn left and follow Georgeson Bay Road to Montague Harbour Road—a road that terminates at Montague Harbour and the government wharf launch adjacent to a now–unused ferry slip. There is parking available on the road above the dock.

During the summer months, the road to the government wharf may be congested with traffic, making access to this particular launch site difficult. If this is the case, use the public ramp at Montague Harbour Marine Park. There is ample parking adjacent to this launch site.

The Route

Prior to launching, paddlers may wish to visit the Montague Harbour Marina. The operators run a small store. During the summer season a small café that overlooks the water is open to the public. Gulf Island Sea Kayaking, a long time rental and tour business also operates here.

Intricate features in these sandstone cliffs were carved by the sea. Photo: Dave Pinel.

From the launch, head directly to the channel between Parker Island and Gray Peninsula, as many of the features attractive to paddlers are located outside the confines of this sheltered harbour.

Gray Peninsula is part of the Gulf Islands National Park Reserve – Montague Harbour Park, and immediately upon rounding the easternmost point of this landmark, you will see a beautiful sand beach, one of several beaches in the park. This may be a little too soon for a rest stop, but for those leaving the harbour, this spot serves well as a stopover.

Two sandy coves are found on either side of the low isthmus on Parker Island. Paddle along the outer shoreline of the tiny islets west of Parker, paying particular attention to

the faster–moving currents between the east point of Wise Island and the offshore islet. Oystercatchers are typically seen on this tiny rock outcrop. All of the islets in this area are privately owned.

For years the dead junipers on the tiny Ballingal Islets were recognized as unique nesting site for the double–crested cormorants. In 1963 the islets received provincial park status in order to maximize protection for the nesting site. Unfortunately over decades the numbers of nesting pairs declined rapidly. In 1957 there were 74 nests, 25 in 1987, and in 1993 three were left. By the late 90s there were no active nests remaining. The decline is likely due to both human disturbance and the rise in the number of bald eagles. Nesting cormorants react to both eagles and humans in the same way—if either comes close the adults will fly off leaving the eggs vulnerable to predation. Weather has now taken it's toll on these once remarkable tree nests.

Southwest Shore of Galiano

From the Ballingal Islets, head shoreward. The waterfront along the most obvious cliff face is well worth exploring. Large sandstone grottos have been carved out at the base of 60 m– (200 ft–) high bluffs. Pelagic cormorants live highrise style on the narrow ledges, and at sea level various intertidal creatures are both colourful and plentiful and are best observed at low tide.

The only pebble beach, easily accessed by paddlers along this section of the route, is located east of these impressive cliffs. A public access from shoreward may mean sharing the space with others, but the locals are not only friendly but in my experience also quite informative.

At this stage paddlers may choose to follow Galiano's shores up toward Retreat Cove in order to link up with trip 20, Wallace Island Marine Park or trip 23, Valdes Island. The distance to Retreat Cove is a little over 2 nmi. It's an additional 5 nmi to North Galiano's Spanish Hills' government wharf.

For those choosing to return to Montague Harbour, follow the shoreline closely as it is made interesting by a number of unusual sandstone shapes carved by wave erosion. Most impressive is a natural carving referred to by locals as Mushroom Rock.

Sandstones of the Strait

Even a brief look at a chart of the Gulf Islands region shows a characteristic alignment of the islands, whose shapes are generally elongated from northwest to southeast. The islands are the eroded crests and edges of sedimentary rock layers that were compressed into a series of parallel folds millions of years ago by tectonic forces acting from the southwest.

All the sandstones you see in this region are part of the Nanaimo Group, a sequence of deposits totaling over 16 km (10 mi) in thickness. These layers include conglomerates, coal seams, shales and sandstones that underlie most of Vancouver Island's east coast, in addition to forming most of the Gulf Islands.

The spectacular erosive features seen in these rocks have all been created since glacial ice last disappeared from the Strait of Georgia about 13,000 years ago. The silica and calcite cements that bind the particles of quartz and other minerals in sandstone are easily dissolved by sea water. Wherever waves act on softer zones of these rocks, erosion is accelerated, producing intricate "fretted" or "honeycombed" outcrops. Especially impressive are the major overhanging "galleries"—some of which were used by early Spanish explorers in this area to cache provisions. Post–glacial "rebound" of the region over several thousand years gradually lifted some of the sculptured cliffs above the reach of the waves.

Legend tells of concealed caves along this Galiano shore and secret passages climbing to exits on bluffs above Montague Harbour. Remember the murder that took place at Murder Point on the southern shores of Saturna in the 1860s? (If not, the story is told in trip 10.) Apparently, the party guilty of committing the crime hid in these caves until the leader of the assailants was discovered.

Garry oak, juniper, arbutus and Douglas fir, all drought adaptive, grace the cliffs along this shore. Even the prickly pear cactus grows on these south–facing shores. Interestingly, Galiano is one of the driest of all the Gulf Islands, receiving a mere 80 cm (32 in) of rain a year.

What makes paddling so exceptional from the fall through the spring are the countless birds that over–winter in this area. In fact, most paddlers will likely encounter at least a dozen species during a day's excursion in the off–season. In the early fall, both arctic and common loons return to these waters, along with huge numbers of surf and common scooters. These are quickly followed by the returning Barrow's and common goldeneye. During the winter, the three mergansers—hooded, common and red–headed—are found, along with grebes, buffleheads and scaups, while in the spring, the mergansers and loons, now in full breeding plumage, are joined by migratory Brandt's geese. Hummingbirds, drawn to the warmth of south–facing bluffs, return to the cliffs early each spring.

Expect to see several resident eagles, blue herons, kingfishers, pigeon guillemots and oystercatchers—all of them year–round inhabitants.

Montague Harbour

Montague Harbour Marine Park was the first marine park established in BC (1959) and to this day remains very popular with pleasure boaters. It has earned a reputation as being the busiest of all the marine parks —the park has a wharf and several mooring buoys and is also accessible to car campers. For this reason, many paddlers may wish to pass it over during the summer months. However, in June and September you could well expect no one else to be using the several walk–in locations that are located well away from car–accessible sites. The park charges a per party camping fee—$17 in 2004. Check the BC Parks website for current rates at www.bcparks.ca.

As you paddle the shoreline along the north side of the park, note the white–shell beach. This entire stretch of shore was inhabited from almost three thousand years ago to the arrival of white men by natives, who over the countless years of occupation discarded the shells that form the midden. Storms have subsequently eroded the beach, leaving the shell fragments visible today.

Perhaps the only difficulty paddlers will have in this area is a mental one stimulated by the half–dozen powerlines that manage to cross just about every beach and cove on Gray Peninsula and Parker Island. Passing 38 m (125 ft) overhead, they are certainly not a navigational hazard, but the sight of them is rather irksome.

6 Sansum Narrows

Nowhere in the Gulf Islands does an area represent the steep fiords typical of the Pacific coast more accurately than the Sansum Narrows. Paddle the narrows under 2,300 foot bluffs. Watch as turkey vultures and eagles ride the thermals. Peer into the eel grass shallows for a glimpse of the carnivorous moonsnail. Complete your visit with a meal or a pint of beer at any one of a number of seaside cafes and pubs.

Harbour Seals are a common sight in the Gulf Islands. Photo: Kelly Irving.

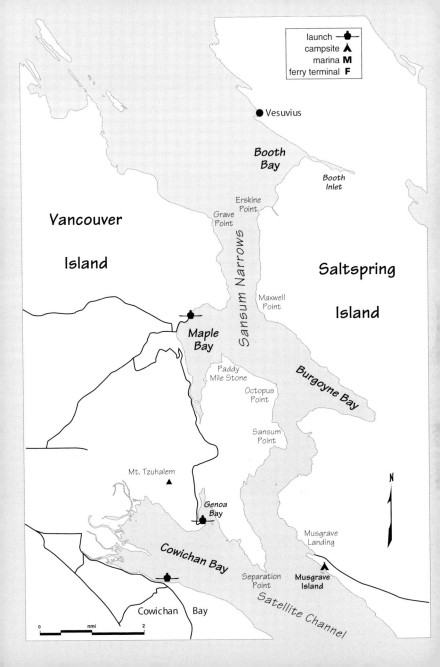

launch ⬟
campsite ⚊
marina **M**
ferry terminal **F**

● Vesuvius

Booth
Bay

Booth
Inlet

Erskine
Point

Grave
Point

Vancouver

Island

Sansum Narrows

Maxwell
Point

Saltspring

Island

Maple
Bay

Paddy
Mile Stone

Burgoyne Bay

Octopus
Point

Sansum
Point

Mt. Tzuhalem
▲

Genoa
Bay

Musgrave
Landing

Cowichan Bay

Separation
Point

Musgrave
Island
▲

N

Cowichan   Bay

Satellite Channel

0   nmi   2

16 Cowichan Bay to Musgrave Landing

Difficulty Beginner conditions – low risk
Distance 6 nmi round trip
Duration Day trip or overnight
Charts 3441 Haro Strait, Boundary Pass and Satellite Channel (1:40,000)
Tides Reference Port: Fulford Harbour
Secondary Ports: Maple Bay and Cowichan Bay
Currents Reference Station: Active Pass
Secondary Station: Sansum Narrows
Camping Musgrave Island
Land Jurisdictions Crown Land – Musgrave Island and adjacent shoreline

What makes this paddle so delightful is exploring a little–known reserve area on Saltspring Island. Wander through open meadows where sheep contentedly graze, and follow a bubbling creek to a secluded waterfall, then camp in the coolness of a forest–sheltered site behind Musgrave Island.

Paddling Considerations

Both Cowichan Bay and Satellite Channel are open to occasional afternoon winds that are at times quite fresh. Currents are strongest between Separation Point and Musgrave Landing. In my experience, the Current Atlas provides the most accurate representation of flows in Sansum Narrows, although they can also be predicted by using the Tide and Current Tables. Chop may result when currents flowing out of the narrows meet opposing winds from Satellite Channel.

Given the predictability of these considerations this route is suited to the beginner paddler.

Getting There and Launching

To access the Cowichan Bay launch, follow Highway 1 north from Victoria or if coming from Nanaimo take Highway 1 south. Just south of Duncan, take the Cowichan Bay turnoff, and follow Cowichan Bay Road to Cowichan Bay. There is a public boat ramp and plenty of parking space less than a kilometer north of this seaside community. Allow an hour to drive from Victoria to Cowichan Bay and an hour and a half from Nanaimo.

The Route

Paddle the northern shoreline of Cowichan Bay, or head straight across the bay to Separation Point. This 2 nmi crossing can be affected by brisk southeasterlies, as can the 1 nmi Sansum Narrows crossing. Check weather conditions prior to paddling these open waters.

Having crossed to Saltspring, look for a dilapidated government wharf within the confines of the delightfully secluded Musgrave Landing. This previously isolated area is changing as the southern point has been subdivided, and a mooring dock associated

Launching from Cowichan Bay. Photo: David Spittlehouse.

with the development now assumes much space in the cove.

But the main attraction that makes Musgrave Landing a worthwhile destination is a short walk away. Beach kayaks and take the road from the wharf up to the main gravel road. Turn right to make a gentle upward climb. Within about 8 to 10 minutes look to the right for an overgrown roadway leading into a greenbelt reserve—an area set aside for public recreation use (There are no signs indicating this is a greenbelt area.) These 34 ha (87 ac) were once used as a farm; sheep continue to roam the open pastures. Pass through the meadows, following a rough trail that eventually drops down into a creek bed. A short distance upstream, a secluded waterfall cascades into a crystal–clear pool.

The surrounding rain forest provides a magnificent backdrop for falls that are most impressive in the spring.

Retrace your route back to the main gravel road. As you begin your descent back to Musgrave Landing, look to the left for another overgrown trail. Follow it down to a pebble beach that faces out to a tiny island known locally as Musgrave Island. There is a campsite in the forest above the shore. It is my understanding that some locals have received permission to set up a rudimentary campsite on this parcel of crown land. Upon returning to the kayaks beached at Musgrave paddlers can return to Cowichan Bay or follow the shoreline to spend the night at the campsite behind Musgrave Island.

17 Maple Bay To Genoa Bay

Difficulty Beginner conditions – low risk
Distance 8 nmi – one way
Duration Day trip
Charts 3441 Haro Strait, Boundary Pass and Satellite Channel (1:40,000)
Tides Reference Port: Fulford Harbour
Secondary Ports: Maple Bay and Cowichan Bay
Currents Reference Station: Active Pass
Secondary Station: Sansum Narrows
Camping No camping
Land Jurisdictions Not applicable

Schedule paddling so as to take advantage of the free ride offered by currents in fiord–like Sansum Narrows. Falcons and eagles soar above precipitous cliffs, and secluded coves offer enchanting rest stops. Don't miss the Genoa Bay Marina, undoubtedly one of the most charming in all the Gulf Islands.

Paddling Considerations

The currents through Sansum Narrows occasionally reach up to 3 knots; therefore, paddle from north to south with an ebb tide and from south to north with a flood.

Southerly winds tend to funnel through the narrows, and at times can affect progress. When these winds meet an opposing ebb current, light chop is likely to occur at the south end of the narrows.

Although currents reach up to 3 knots these are predictable and with scheduling are avoided. This route is suited to beginner paddlers who can schedule paddling with the tide and who have determined that the marine weather broadcasts indicate favourable conditions.

Getting There and Launching

If paddling south, launch from Maple Bay. Launch from Genoa Bay if paddling north. A one–way paddle requires leaving a vehicle at either launch, but it only takes ten minutes to drive from Maple Bay to Genoa Bay.

To access the Maple Bay launch take Highway 1 to Duncan. From the centre of town follow the signs to Maple Bay. Make a left turn onto Beaumont Avenue and within several hundred meters look for the Maple Bay Rowing Club. Launch from the public ramp adjacent to the club. A large parking area provides ample space to leave vehicles.

To access the Genoa Bay launch follow the same route as outlined for Maple Bay, only prior to reaching Maple Bay, take the well–marked Genoa Bay turnoff. The winding gravel road terminates at Genoa Bay where paddlers may launch from the Genoa Bay Marina. The proprietors do not charge a fee for the use of the adjacent lot but tell them of your intentions.

The Route

The route is described as though paddled from Maple Bay to Genoa Bay.

Paddle the perimeter of Maple Bay to Paddy Mile Stone. From here to Octopus Point the shallows support an eel–grass environment. Look closely as eel grass provides shelter for many animals from microscopic life forms to larger creatures such as crabs, moonsnails and limpets. Diatoms are microscopic organisms that, if present in large enough numbers, constitute the furry olive–brown coating that covers the eel grass leaves. The tangled mat of grass is also teeming with small fish.

Consider a side trip to Burgoyne Bay. Mount Maxwell looms 595 m (1,952 ft) above the bay—an excellent place to watch turkey vultures, bald eagles and human hang gliders. The government wharf at the head of the bay provides access to Saltspring. Stroll along an idyllic country road that winds inland past several of Saltspring's sheep farms.

Sansum Point marks the entrance to a channel that is as close to a coastal fiord as could ever be found in the Gulf Islands. Steep rock bluffs rise up from the narrows to 690 m (2300 ft) Bruce Peak on Saltspring Island and 240 m (800 ft) Stoney Hill on Vancouver Island. Eagles and vultures soar above these impressive cliffs.

Burial Islet, so named as it served as a native burial ground, offers little in the way of alluring stopovers, but it is an excellent shoreline to follow as, at low tide, the intertidal life here is quite remarkable. Especially beautiful are the white plumose anemones. These gorgeous metridiums take on quite a different appearance at low tide when the feathery tentacles, visible at high tide, are retracted. All that remains is a drooping, slimy stalk.

A rocky shoreline from Sansum Point to Separation Point discourages landing. A single gravel beach just north of Separation Point point provides the only shore access. Rounding Separation Point may require crossing eddylines, and if winds from Satellite Channel meet an opposing ebb tide, expect steep waves in this area.

Several shell and gravel beaches break up the rocky shore between Separation Point and Genoa Bay. The large bight located halfway along this stretch of coast has a sheltered pebble beach fronting a large grassy meadow. The driftwood lean–tos, fire pits and makeshift benches all testify to its popularity.

Genoa Bay Marina is truly one of the most charming in all the Gulf Islands. The cafe, where a casual and friendly atmosphere is immediately apparent, leans out over the water and looks down on an assortment of seaworthy craft from houseboats to fishing boats. Don't miss this opportunity for a delicious meal.

Looking to stretch those cockpit–confined muscles? A short walk up the main Genoa Bay road connects hikers to a footpath that winds its way out to Skinner Point. The trail continues on to Skinner Bluff, then up to the 510 m (1700 ft) peak of Mount Tzuhalem. The route is steep, but the views of surrounding Gulf Islands are magnificent. Allow at least an hour to get to the top.

Steep rock bluffs line the shore of Sansum Narrows. Photo: David Spittlehouse.

18 Maple Bay to Vesuvius

Difficulty Beginner conditions – low risk
Distance 10 nmi round trip
Duration Day trip
Charts 3441 Haro Strait, Boundary Pass and Satellite Channel (1:40,000)
Tides Reference Port: Fulford Harbour
Secondary Port: Maple Bay
Currents Reference Station: Active Pass
Secondary Station: Sansum Narrows
Camping No camping
Land Jurisdictions Not applicable

Launch from a delightful seaside community, and paddle beneath the towering peaks that contribute to the fiord–like appearance of Sansum Narrows. Cross open waters at the entrance to Booth Bay, or enter a fascinating marine environment found within Booth Inlet. And don't miss Vesuvius—a tiny Saltspring community that boasts a delightful waterside pub complete with a balcony where paddlers can indulge in sumptuous pub fare prior to returning home.

Paddling Considerations

Currents in this section of Sansum Narrows seldom exceed 1.5 knots; however, paddlers may wish to co-ordinate a northward paddle with a flood and a southward paddle with the ebb. (Although the chart indicates flows of 3 knots, the Current Atlas provides the most accurate representation of current flows in this part of the narrows, indicating that flows do not exceed 1.5 knots.)

Southerly winds do affect these waters, but during the summer, waves rarely build to a significant height.

Generally these considerations indicate a route suited to beginners however given the 2 nmi open stretch across the entrance to Booth Bay it would be best to have experienced paddlers in the group. (This open stretch is avoided by paddling the shoreline, but that increases the return trip length to 14 nmi.)

Getting There and Launching

Follow the same directions for the Maple Bay launch described in trip 17, Maple Bay to Genoa Bay.

The Route

Launch from Maple Bay's public boat ramp. Some paddlers may wish to wander up to the waterside pub located a couple hundred meters north of the launch.

From the launch, follow rocky shoreline to Arbutus Point, then cross the 0.5 nmi–wide Sansum Narrows, navigating toward Maxwell Point. From here the northward stretch along isolated shores is particularly beautiful as little development has occurred on this part of Saltspring. Rock bluffs rise from the sea to grass–patched ledges where elevated knolls support Garry oak and arbutus forests. In the spring these dry coastal woodlands abound with the colour of blossoming wildflowers. A gravel beach just south of Erskine Point provides the best place to land.

For the shortest paddling distance to Vesuvius, leave Erskine Point and traverse the waters at the entrance to Booth Bay, an open crossing of 2 nmi.

An extended route follows the entire shoreline of Booth Bay, along which is found Arbutus Beach. Here the creek draining Lake Maxwell empties into the sea. An expansive sand and gravel beach surrounding the outfall provides easy access and an excellent lunch stop. However, as this area is accessible by road, expect to share this spot with Saltspring residents, especially on a sunny summer day.

Continue on to the entrance to Booth Inlet, easily distinguished by the sandbar that flanks its south shore. This inlet is best explored at high tide (at low tide gumboots may be required). During peak floods, the water that rushes through the narrow entrance provides an exhilarating ride. However, the waters inside the inlet are calm. Even the shore birds are silent as they probe the silt. Within the confined waters, pungent salty odours fill the air. The paddle concludes at the bridge, as beyond it the water is too shallow for passage. From here, the town of Ganges is only 2 km (1.2 mi), a distance that island residents considered dredging so as to join Booth Bay to Ganges Harbour.

Turn back to the head of Booth Bay and the 1 nmi paddle to Vesuvius.

Vesuvius is a delightful seaside village with an idyllic location and waterside facilities that certainly make it a worthwhile destination point. Two locations provide landing access, the government wharf and a nearby beach. Space is limited at the single–float government dock, but if there is room, this access is closest to nearby facilities. The beach at the head of Vesuvius Bay has a stairway leading to Langley Street. Follow it to Vesuvius Bay Road, then turn left to access a well–known Gulf Islands stopover—the Vesuvius pub. This very popular watering hole operates above the government wharf and not only provides brew but also serves excellent pub fare in a relaxed West Coast atmosphere. And don't miss a visit to the Vesuvius Bay General Store as this tiny establishment, located a few hundred metres up Vesuvius Bay Road, is one of those remarkable country stores that stocks just about everything.

The Vesuvius Queen docks at the adjacent ferry slip. She is one of the smallest of the Gulf Islands ferry fleet, carrying commuters from Saltspring to Crofton. The wash from her wake is not a threat, but paddlers should note that she moves in and out of the slip not only quickly but also frequently.

Cross from Erskine Point to Grave Point on the return trip. The route southward from Grave Point passes uninhabited shorelines, and the steep cliffs behind rise up to 510 m (1700 ft) Maple Mountain.

7 Central Gulf Islands

These easy weekend paddles presents many high-lights. Bask in the sun on an alluring sand–fringed bay on Tent Island. Or spend a lazy afternoon on Wallace Island. Follow an undulating, forest–lined trail and wander past rusting farm implements that lie in testimony to previous inhabitants. At the day's end, watch the moon rise through the arbutus canopy from an elevated headland at Chivers Point.

Campsite at Conover Cove, Wallace Island. Photo: Andrew Madding.

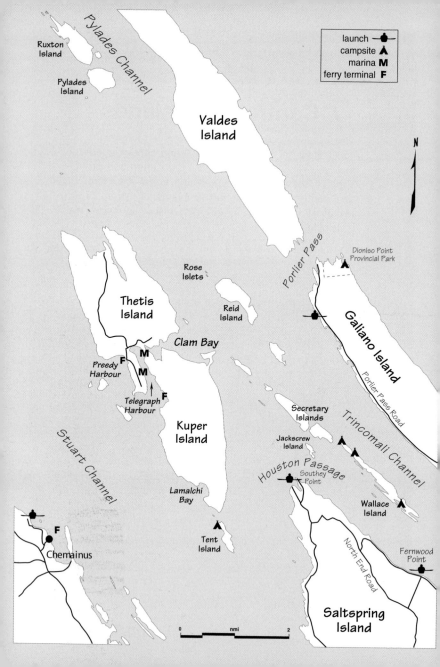

Ruxton Island

Pylades Channel

Pylades Island

Valdes Island

launch ⚓
campsite ⚑
marina M
ferry terminal F

N

Rose Islets

Thetis Island

Reid Island

Porlier Pass

Dioniso Point Provincial Park

Galiano Island

Clam Bay

F

M

M

Preedy Harbour

F

Telegraph Harbour

Kuper Island

Stuart Channel

Secretary Islands

Trincomali Channel

Jackscrew Island

Houston Passage

Porlier Pass Road

Southey Point

Wallace Island

Lamalchi Bay

Tent Island

Chemainus

F

North End Road

Fernwood Point

Saltspring Island

0   nmi   2

19 Thetis, Kuper, Tent and Reid Islands

Difficulty Beginner conditions – low risk
Distance 15 nmi round trip
Duration 2 –3 days
Chart 3442 – North Pender to Thetis Island (1:40,000)
Tides Reference Port: Fulford Harbour
Secondary Ports: Preedy Harbour and Chemainus
Currents Reference Station: Race Passage
Secondary Station: Trincomali Channel
Camping Tent Island (only with permission from the Penelakuts)
Wallace Island Marine Park (Trip 20)
Galiano Island – Dionisio Point Provincial Park (Trip 23)
Land Jurisdictions BC Parks – Wallace Island and Dionisio Point Provincial Park.
Indian Reserve – Tent Island

Here is a delightful route that is easily paddled in a weekend by leaving Thetis early Friday evening, camping on Tent Island Friday night, spending Saturday night camped on Wallace Island and returning to Thetis by Sunday afternoon.

Don't miss the pelagic cormorant colonies on cliff faces along Kuper and Tent Islands', beautiful sand–fringed bays on Tent and the remains of a Japanese saltery on Reid Island.

Paddling Considerations
During the summer, winds in this area are usually calm, although waters are occasionally affected by southeasters blowing up Trincomali and Stuart Channels.

Paddlers may choose to ride a flood when heading north and the ebb when heading south, but for the most part, currents are minimal. The only turbulence due to tidal flows is found off Southey Point during peak floods and ebbs.

Beginner paddlers who have listened to wind forecasts and know that southeasters are not likely to affect these waters will enjoy the favourable paddling conditions in this area. (The 3 nmi crossing of Stuart Channel is easily avoided by novice paddlers by taking the ferry to Thetis Island.)

Getting There and Launching
Launch from one of two launch locations – Chemainus on Vancouver Island or Preedy Harbour on Thetis Island.

To access the Chemainus launch, follow Highway 1 from either Victoria or Nanaimo. Turn off the highway to Chemianus just north of Duncan, following signs to Chemainus and the Thetis–Kuper ferry. The route eventually heads down Oak Street through the "old town" part of Chemainus. Turn left onto Esplanade, and follow it around to Kin Park. Launch from the ramp adjacent to the park. There is no parking available here—park your vehicles on a nearby street.

To access Thetis Island's Preedy Harbour launch, follow the same route as for the Chemainus launch, but follow Oak Street down to the Thetis–Kuper Island ferry terminal. Board the ferry with vehicles, or unload gear and walk on. An area just ahead and to the left of the ferry lineup provides space to unload. The launch on Thetis Island's Preedy Harbour is adjacent to the ferry slip. Look to the left for a short trail leading to the pebble beach launch upon leaving the ferry. Vehicles can be left parked on the road above the ferry dock.

The Route

If you haven't seen the murals painted on many of the buildings in the town of Chemainus, they are a worthwhile side trip. And if last minute provisions are required, there is a general store close to the Thetis–Kuper ferry terminal. The Chemainus bakery, two blocks up from the terminal, has an irresistible selection of baked goods.

Crossing the open waters of Stuart Channel (3 nmi) in the summer is straightforward as winds are usually calm (watch for occasional southeasters) and currents in the channel are minimal. Navigate toward Active Point at the approximate centre of Kuper Island. On the horizon Kuper appears flatter than the somewhat hilly Thetis Island.

Paddlers launching from Preedy Harbour will note that, although the foreshore on the south end of Thetis is developed, paddling along these shores is most pleasant.

Kuper Island

Kuper Island is an Indian reserve, and except for the village at the north end of the island and the ferry terminal on Telegraph Harbour, it remains relatively natural. Paddle south toward Augustus Point. Here pelagic cormorants nest on the narrow cliff ledges.

Lamalchi Bay is named after a Cowichan tribe who originally lived at the south end of Kuper. A village once stood on the bay. However, due to drastic population reductions in the late 1800s (due to smallpox and tuberculosis), the few remaining Lamalchis amalgamated with the Penelakuts at the north end of Kuper. The only piece of land on Kuper Island not included in the reserve is on Lamalchi Bay. It was not included when the reserve boundaries were set in 1916 because it was the site of a church founded by the North American Society for the Propagation of the Gospel.

Tent Island

Tent Island is owned by the Penelakut Band on Kuper Island. The Penelakuts generously allow camping on Tent however permission must be obtained beforehand. Call the band office at 250–246–2321. The band will ask for a small donation. (See "Reserve Lands" in this book's introduction for further information.) Paddlers will quickly discover the area is very popular with boaters who moor in the large bay on the west side of Tent. You may wish to head to a secluded sand beach (just north of the popular moorage) where there is ample space for several tents in the arbutus forest above. (Avoid a view

Moonsnails

No other snail could possibly be confused with this one. It's huge! The shell itself is up to 10 cm (4 in.) wide, and when extended, the immense foot is the size of a dinner plate.

The moonsnail is carnivorous, ploughing along under the surface of the sand in search of clams. Once it finds its food, the moonsnail drills a neat hole through the victim's shell and then sucks out the meaty flesh. Next time you walk a beach littered with clam shells, look closely for the neat hole bored by the moonsnail. Perhaps most unusual is the rubber like collar constructed by the huge snail. First–time viewers are often puzzled by these unique formations as they bear a remarkable resemblance to discarded rubber plungers. In fact, they are an egg case, containing hundreds of thousands of eggs sandwiched between two layers of sand held together by mucous secretions. In mid summer the egg case crumbles and half a million free–swimming larvae are committed to the sea.

Photo: Sherry Kirkvold.

of the smoke from the Crofton pulp mill by choosing a tent location that faces north.)

Paddle the 1.5 mi around Tent Island. Large numbers of moonsnails and their casings are found in the pass between Tent and Kuper, cormorants nest on the cliff edges on the island's southwest end and nearby North Reef is a prime bottom–fishing area. (Look for its well–marked shallows on the chart.)

~

The crossing to Jackscrew Island is 0.5 mi. From here, paddlers may choose to head to a campsite on Wallace Island (see trip 20) or continue northward toward the Secretaries.

The Secretaries appear most inviting with their open arbutus and evergreen woodlands. However, North and South Secretary are privately owned. A sand bank joins the two islands at all but high tide. Appropriately, the native name for the area is Shemetsen, meaning "goes dry." (Rozen) When shellfish harvesting is permitted, the exposed mud flat provides the persevering digger with a sumptuous meal of clams.

The perimeters of Mowgli and Norway Islands are rocky, and the

Looking up Porlier Pass from the tip of Hall Island. Photo: Bob Davidson.

few protected beaches are close to private residences. Land on an un-named bay on the south end of Hall Island—an easily accessed beach stop where a combination of sandy shores and rocky reefs provides interesting exploration. This entire island was at one time owned by Anna Morgan, also named the "Mystery Duchess, Hermit of the Isle of Echoes." She lived in total isolation here from 1907 to 1933 (Wolferstan).

In a previous versoion of this sea kayak guide I recommended camp-ing on a tiny unnamed islet on the southern tip of Reid Island. However several factors lead me to discourage paddlers from doing so now. The first and perhaps most important is recognition of the sensitivity of this tiny ecosystem. As the numbers of kayakers swell these rare unihabited isles are starting to show the impact of frequent stop overs. The second reason is that two parks, created since writing this original book in 1990, are easily accessed in this area – Wallace Island (see trip 20, Wallace island) and Dionisio (trip 23, Valdes Island). The last reason is that the only access to this islet is from the rocky south end where the exposed flat ledges make for very difficult landings.

Reid Island

Reid Island was purchased in 1852 for $2.52 by Joe Silvey, the first Portuguese immigrant in Canada granted British citizenship. The wooded isle is still privately owned but remains largely undeveloped. Plan to stop at the pebble beach in the sheltered bay facing Thetis. Hidden behind the thick blackberry bramble at the south end of this bay are the remains of a Japanese saltery, established here in about 1908. Apparently, this operation employed about 150 men. The dry salt herring shipped from here went to Nanaimo, then on to export markets in the Orient. With the establishment of several other salteries on adjacent islands (Valdes and Galiano), Nanaimo became a major herring centre. Operations peaked in 1910 when 27,800 tons of salt herring were exported. With the relocation of all Japanese during World War II, salteries were shut down. Government legislation disallowed Japanese returning to their confiscated lands, and subsequently fish processing ended here.

Rose Islets

Less than a mile to the north of Reid Island is the Rose Islets, an ecological reserve established in 1971 to protect marine wildlife. In 1968, 180 pairs of double–breasted cormorants nested here. Their numbers have been on the decline since. Other bird species frequenting the Rose group include oystercatchers, harlequin ducks, pigeon guillemots and glaucous–winged gulls.

This highly sensitive seabird nesting site has been declared off limits to visitors.

~

The crossing from the Rose Islets to Clam Bay is just over 1 nmi. Currents are minor. The outstanding white shell–beaches of Penelakut Spit mark the entrance to Clam Bay. (The native community behind is home to Kuper Island's Penelakut tribe.) At one time a traditional village composed of fifteen longhouses stood out on the spit where extended families of up to twenty individuals lived in each house. The Indian word for the village is "Penalexeth," meaning "buried houses on the beach" (Rozen).

The dredged pass between Thetis and Kuper Islands poses little threat to the kayaker. Tidal currents are minimal, flooding east and ebbing west. Some have likened the waterway to an irrigation ditch during low tides. At high tides, soft muddy banks line the shallow passage. The north shore is populated by Thetis Island residents, while native homes dot the Kuper Island side.

Two marinas operate in the sheltered waters of Telegraph Harbour and attract many boaters. Kayakers can stop for groceries, or enjoy the waterfront pub. If you are coordinating your trip with ferry schedules, allow an hour to paddle from the pub to the Preedy Harbour ferry dock. To paddle from Telegraph Harbour to Chemainus, allow approximately two hours.

20 Wallace Island Marine Park

Difficulty Beginner conditions – low risk
Distance 1 nmi – from Saltspring to Wallace Island
6 nmi to circumnavigate Wallace Island
Duration 1 –2 days
Charts 3442 – North Pender to Thetis Island (1:40,000)
Tides Reference Port: Fulford Harbour
Secondary Ports: Crofton and Chemainus
Currents Reference Station: Race Passage
Secondary Station: Trincomali Channel
Camping Wallace Island – Chivers Point, Conover Cove and Cabin Point
Land Jurisdictions BC Parks – Wallace Island

Head out from either of the launches from Saltspring and within an hour arrive at one of the newest of BC's marine parks—Wallace Island. It is little wonder that such colourful historic residents were drawn here. Sheltered coves, offshore islets, a midland trail meandering through juniper, fir and arbutus forests, historical remains and virtually assured glimpses of harbour seals, eagles and otter are only a few of the features that make a visit to this easily accessed island more than worthwhile.

Paddling Considerations

During the summer the waters in Houston Passage off the north end of Saltpring are calm and winds are light. On occasion southeasters may blow up Trincomali Channel. Currents are minimal. The only turbulence due to tidal flows is found off Southey Point during peak floods and ebbs.

Novice paddlers who have listened to wind forecasts and know that southeasters are not likely to affect these waters will enjoy the favourable paddling conditions in this area.

Getting There and Launching

Wallace Island is easily accessed from Southey Point or Fernwood, both on the north end of Saltspring Island. Paddlers board Saltspring–bound ferries at either the Tsawwassen or Swartz Bay terminal. From either of the two Saltspring terminals, follow signs to Ganges. To get to the two launch sites at Southey Point head north from Ganges by following signs to Vesuvius and then to Southey Point via North End Road. Turn right off North End Road onto Southey Point Road to gain access to a sheltered bay launch at the end of this road. Limited roadside parking is possible. A second launch is accessed by turning off Southey Point Road onto Arbutus Road. A short trail leads to a beach at the end of Arbutus Road. Again, limited roadside parking is available.

To get to Fernwood launch, follow the above directions for Southey Point only make a right turn approximately 4 km (2.5 mi) along North End Road (measure from intersection of North End and Vesuvius Bay Roads) onto Fernwood Road. A government wharf where Fernwood Road joins North Beach Road serves as a launch site for Wallace Island. But better yet, head further north along North Beach Road and within a couple of hundred metres there is a steep access to a boat launch. This location provides easy water access and there is parking on North Beach Road.

The Route

This route is described assuming a launch from Southey Point.

Up until recently Wallace Island's alluring coves and forest trails were not accessible to paddlers. Fortunately all but 4 ha (11 ac) were purchased by the province in 1990 and Wallace was declared a park.

Looking north from Wallace Island's Chivers Point. Photo: Stafford Reid.

Wallace Island is not unlike many of the surrounding Gulf Islands in that mild winters are followed by very dry summers. As fire hazards are high, camp fires are not permitted—not even below the high tide line. BC Parks requests that paddlers camp at one of three designated areas—Conover Cove and Chivers and Cabin Points. A minimal user fee applies and is collected on an honour system by depositing in the associated self-registration vault.

Visitors to these shores cannot help but ponder the lives of past residents. Jeremiah Chivers, a retired gold miner, died on the island at the age of ninety–two. All that remains of his solitary thirty–eight–year influence are the twisted fruit trees lining Conover Cove. The American, David Conover, who credits himself for discovering Marilyn Monroe in his autobiographical Finding Marilyn, was full of dreams of an ideal existence when he purchased the island in 1946. Subsequent books, Once Upon an Island and One Man's Island, describe the victories and setbacks of his twenty–year residency. The cabins that remain in Conover Cove were part of Conover Resort, which once included guest cottages, a recreation hall and various support buildings.

A winter paddle to Wallace transported me to a virtually deserted isle. The 1 nmi crossing from Saltspring's Southey Point ended on a secluded beach at Chivers Point. On a summer weekend undoubtedly numerous paddlers would already have settled here, having chosen one of the several tent locations. Up until recently paddlers predictably set up camp on the elevated headlands that define the bay at Chivers Point, understandably drawn to the views of nearby Galiano and Saltspring Islands. However, so that these areas are protected from overuse, BC Parks has wisely set up designated camp locations. Dispersed along the trail, these six forest–sheltered sites offer secluded camping and leave Chivers Point and beaches for the general use of all who visit. Pit toilets are also a part of the recent Parks' development here.

An obvious southward trail will beckon to most visitors. Follow the forest–lined route. In winter expect to see the hoof prints of resident black–tail deer. Within forty minutes this undulating path widens and shortly thereafter spills into an open meadow. Rusting farm implements lay in testimony to previous inhabitants. A water pump, maintained by BC Parks, is located here—however, signs advise boiling this water before drinking it. Carry on and in five minutes the historic buildings associated with Conover Cove come into view. In summer anticipate that many others will be taking advantage of the recreational resources situated around the cove. Good anchorage and a moorage dock understandably attract many boaters. Tent and picnic sites, toilets and visitor services are also available. Solitude–seeking paddlers may choose to pass the cove and follow the right–bearing 1 km (0.6 mi) trail that leads to Panther Point. Eagles, river otter and seals are commonly observed from this quiet promontory.

Cabin Point is the least visited of the three designated camp locations. It is located about half a nautical mile south of Chivers Point on the east side of the island. Its beauty is as alluring as its isolation. A picturesque rocky outcrop defines the western perimeter of a sand–sheltered bay. Little remains of the cabin that once occupied this site. Parks has taken advantage of the level ground associated with it by setting up several designated campsites. Hike past these tent locations and carry on up the bank to the junction of the trail that travels the length of Wallace.

Not all of Wallace Island is within the park. Please respect the private lands located north of Conover Cove on the western shore.

Upon leaving Wallace, paddlers may return to the Southey Point launch or easily link up with other routes, particularly those described in the North Gulf Islands section. It is a short distance from Wallace across to Galiano's Dionisio Point Provincial Park. For a description of Dionisio, see trip 23, Valdes Island.

8 Northern Gulf Islands

This is an area full of highlights attractive to paddlers. There are no ferries here and no commercial facilities. Most notable are three passes: Gabriola Passage, Porlier Pass and Dodd Narrows. Conveying huge volumes of water these plankton rich channels support rich intertidal life, varied marine mammals and dozens of resident and migratory birds. There is the colourful story of Brother XII, and his consort Madame Zee. Finally, the sandstone galleries on the northwest side of Valdes are quite simply the most magnificent in all the Gulf Islands. Steep cliffs intricately carved by wave erosion inspire the imagination as the convoluted shapes take on the look of sea serpents, huge beehives and mushroom–shaped clouds. A day on the water here draws to an end from a campsite overlooking Georgia Strait and the distant Coast Mountains.

Steep cliffs carved by wave erosion on the northwest side of Valdes Island. Photo: Dave Pinel.

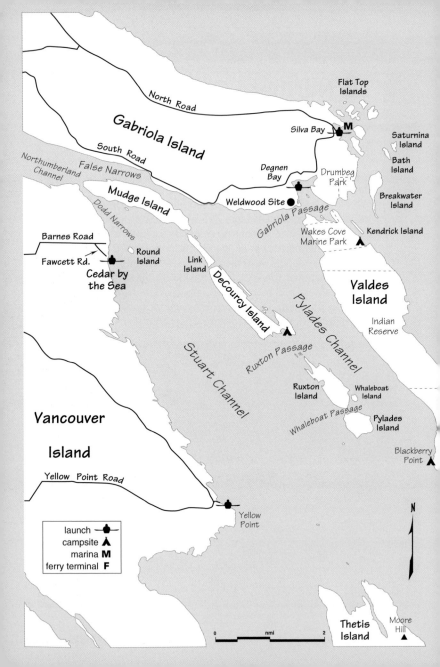

Flat Top
Islands

North Road

Gabriola Island

Silva Bay **M**

Saturnina
Island

South Road

Bath
Island

False Narrows

Degnen
Bay

Drumbeg
Park

Breakwater
Island

Northumberland
Channel

Mudge Island

Weldwood Site ●

Gabriola Passage

Barnes Road

Dodd Narrows

Wakes Cove
Marine Park

Kendrick Island **▲**

Fawcett Rd.

Round
Island

Cedar by
the Sea

Link
Island

DeCourcy Island

Valdes
Island

Indian
Reserve

Pylades Channel

Vancouver

Island

Stuart Channel

Ruxton Passage **▲**

Ruxton
Island

Whaleboat
Island

Whaleboat Passage

Pylades
Island

Yellow Point Road

Blackberry
Point **▲**

Yellow
Point **▲**

launch	●
campsite	**▲**
marina	**M**
ferry terminal	**F**

N

0   nmi   2

Thetis
Island

Moore
Hill **▲**

21 De Courcy Group – Link, De Courcy, Ruxton, and Pylades Islands

Difficulty Beginner conditions – low risk
Distance 12 nmi round trip
Duration 2 days
Charts 3443 Thetis Island to Nanaimo (1:40,000)
Tides Reference Port: Fulford Harbour
Secondary Port: Degnen Bay
Currents No Reference or Secondary Current Stations. (The closest Reference Station is Dodd Narrows and closest Secondary Station is Trincomali Channel.)
Camping DeCourcy Island – Pirates Cove Marine Park
Land Jurisdictions BC Parks – Pirates Cove Marine Park and Whaleboat Island

If the shores along this route could talk, we would hear of Brother XII and his bizarre religious cult, of buried gold and smuggling, even of brainwashing and strange disappearances. The tales would be made all the more colourful by absurd place names like "The City Of Refuge," "Gospel Cove" and the "Fortress For The Future," all areas ruled by the preposterous Brother and his whip–wielding consort, Madame Zee. Brother XII disappeared from the islands more than fifty years ago, yet these places remain much the same today. There are no ferries here and no commercial facilities. The few summer homes found along these shores exist without electric power and telephone service. A quiet ambience prevails in this little–developed archipelago.

Paddling Considerations
This route is the only one in the north Gulf Islands that does not require paddling through one of three major passes within the north Gulf Islands area. Currents are minimal (although paddlers may wish to coordinate paddling north with a flood and south with an ebb), and except for occasional southeasters blowing up Trincomali and evening westerlies, winds are usually calm. (Paddlers should, however, listen to wind predictions prior to heading out.) The only notable turbulence occurs during maximum ebbs in the waters surrounding Round Island and around tiny islets in Ruxton Passage.

Given the favourable paddling conditions that are usually found in this area, the route is suited to the beginner paddler.

Getting There and Launching
This route is accessed from one of two Vancouver island launch sites, Yellow Point and Cedar–by–the–Sea.

Access the Yellow Point launch from either Victoria of Nanaimo by following Highway 1 to north of Ladysmith. Turn off at Cedar Road, following signs for Cedar, Harmac and Yellow Point. Leave Cedar Road at the Yellow Point turnoff. Follow Yellow Point Road to about 0.5 km (0.3 mi) north of Yellow Point Lodge where you turn onto Westby Road and enter Blue Heron Park. Leave vehicles in the adjacent parking area, and launch from the park's beach.

Access the Cedar–by–the–Sea launch by following Highway 1 to just north of Ladysmith. Turn off Cedar Road, and follow signs for Cedar, Harmac, and Yellowpoint for approximately 12 kms to McMillan Road. Turn right on McMillan and within half a km right again on Holden–Corso Road. Follow Holden–Corso for 2 km to Barnes Road. Follow Barnes Road for about 2 km to Fawcett Road. Turn right and drive down Fawcett to its terminus. Launch from the public boat ramp, leaving vehicles parked along Fawcett Road.

If you are heading to the Cedar–by–the Sea launch from Nanaimo leave the city centre by heading south along Nichol Street. Just outside the city limits Nicol becomes the Trans Canada Hi–way. Within a few kilometers you will come to a well–marked intersection with Cedar Road. Turn left and follow Cedar Road for just over 4 kms to McMillan Road. Turn right onto McMillan and within 300 meters turn left onto Holden–Corso Road. Follow Holden–Corso for 2 km to Barnes Road. Follow Barnes Road for about 2 km to Fawcett Road. Turn right and drive down Fawcett to its terminus. Launch from the public boat ramp, leaving vehicles parked along Fawcett Road.

Allow and hour and a half to drive from Victoria to these launches, half an hour from Nanaimo.

The Route
This route is described assuming a Cedar–by–the–Sea launch.

Launch from Cedar–By–The–Sea, a seaside community that was once the headquarters for the Aquarian Foundation (1927) before Brother XII moved the colony to De Courcy Island.

Embark on a Stuart Channel crossing by heading toward Round Island and then crossing from Round Island to the north end of Link Island (1 mi). As currents in the northern sections of Stuart Channel are influenced by flows in Dodd Narrows, paddlers can expect increased tidal flows in this area. Watch for eddylines off of south and east sides of Round Island during a strong ebb.

Link and Mudge Islands
Link and Mudge Islands are actually joined by an extensive shell beach (tombolo). This picturesque tombolo is made up of two U–shaped coves mirroring each other. A shellfish recreation reserve permits the harvesting of the bountiful clams and oysters in the east–facing bay (except in the summer, when the area is most often closed because of PSP).

On a May visit, I was awed by the presence of an industrious group of Vietnamese clam diggers who, over several hours, raked baby clams from the intertidal zone. The harvest was packed into 20 kg (50 lb) sacks and loaded into nearby skiffs, whereupon the combined weight of clams and clam diggers left only a few centimetres of freeboard. I was informed later that an opening for clam harvesting was declared that

Blackberry Point Campsite, Valdes island. Photo: Andrew Madding.

morning. I had just witnessed a day's work for the itinerant crew.

In an emergency the extensive tombolo beach might serve as a camp location as it is below the high tide line. However, locals have observed a number of paddlers camped on the oh–so–tempting meadows immediately above high tide lines. These lands are private and must be respected as such. In a previous edition of this book I erroneously described the unnamed islet on the east side of the tombolo as a suitable camp location. This islet is deeded to Link Island and is private property and not to be used by paddlers. Carry on to Pirate's Cove Marine Park or Blackberry Point on Valdes Island for an overnight stay.

Paddle south along the west sides of Link and De Courcy, passing eroded sandstone cliffs. Convoluted rock and honey–combed hollows result as the sea relentlessly carves the sandstone face. These cliffs jut up from the sea so abruptly that it is easy to get in for a close–up look. Photographers especially will delight at the shadows cast in the evening light. The narrow passage between Link and De Courcy is appropriately called "Hole in the Wall." The narrow gap dries at low tide.

Brother XII

Of all the offbeat religions that seem to flourish on the Pacific coast, there was none quite so bizarre as the Aquarian Foundation led by the notorious Brother XII. Somehow this preposterous guru (his real name was Edward Wilson) convinced intelligent, wealthy people from all over the world to come and join him in building a "Fortress for the Future" in the northern Gulf Islands.

In 1928 notable individuals flocked to the Aquarian base at Cedar–By–The–Sea James Lippincott of Lippincott Publishing Company; Maurice Von Platten, a millionaire pipe–organ builder from Chicago; and Will Comfort, a writer from the Saturday Evening Post. Mary Connally left the affluent social circles of North Carolina and turned over all her life savings to the Foundation so that it was able to purchase De Courcy Islands. Here, the disciples began the arduous task of creating a self–sufficient colony. Greenhouses, orchards, storehouses and even a sawmill were constructed by the loyal followers.

Early on there was dissension among the Aquarians—especially upon the arrival of Isis. (Isis, formerly Mrs. Baumgartner, was convinced by Wilson that she was the reincarnation of the ancient fertility goddess and that she was destined to join him in holy union to create the new messiah.) Wilson, who had systematically bugged the entire colony, was able to pick up every expression of disloyalty. Dissenters were not only identified but were also quoted word for word. Awed by their leader's supposed supernatural powers, they were hushed.

Then there was the most absurd character of all—Madame Zee. Formerly Mrs. Skottowe, a banker's widow from Saskatchewan, she was introduced to the colony as the Brother's right hand. She promptly began overseeing the already overworked colonists. Mary Connally, the Aquarian who had so generously bought the De Courcys, suffered the most under this whip–wielding tyrant.

The Brother and the rather fiendish Zee headed to England where they purchased the *Lady Royal*, a 22 m (72 ft) trawler. Sailing without auxiliary engines, they returned to the Gulf Islands a year later. Several colonists had become used to a more relaxed existence, and when they expressed their dissatisfaction at the Brother's return, they were subsequently banished. In an attempt to regain money invested in the colony, these expatriates filed suit against their former guru. Incredible tales collected over the previous six years were disclosed in court.

Before the trial was completed, the diabolical pair mysteriously disappeared. A newspaper entry printed in 1934 in Switzerland tells of the Brother's probable end. It noted that Julian Skottowe had died. Brother XII, who presumably took the name of Zee's first husband, was buried in Neuchatel. No trace of Madame Zee was ever found.

138 – Sea Kayak the Gulf Islands

De Courcy Island

Whereas the western shore of Link is devoid of housing, the western shore of De Courcy is not. Several summer homes are tucked into the forest above the sandstone ledges. Those interested in the history of the Brother XII colony will want to look at the homestead about halfway along this shore. The barn and orchard were apparently once part of cult operations. (Respect the privacy of the current owners by observing these buildings from the water.)

Paddlers may choose to turn left at the south end of De Courcy Island and head directly to Pirate's Cove Marine Park (described later). Others may wish to explore Ruxton and Pylades Islands. If so, cross the 0.5 nmi–wide Ruxton Passage. Current are minimal except in shallow waters between the drying reefs of the northernmost finger on Ruxton. An inviting shell beach at the head of Herring Bay is often blocked from view as during the summer this bay often fills with boats.

Ruxton and Pylades Islands

Ruxton is subdivided but remains largely undeveloped. Steep sandstone cliffs along the western shore increase in height from north to south. Garry oaks, arbutus and cormorants are found wherever they can grab a foothold. In spring these cliffs are splashed with the orange of Indian paintbrush.

Tiny Tree Island is most inviting, but even though it is uninhabited, it is private land. Exploring above the high tide line is trespassing, so limit your stops to one of several white–shell beaches. There is a shell midden in the cove facing Pylades Island.

Rocky shoreline, steep topography and a thick forest do not tempt a stopover on Pylades Island. The only landing is on the island's northeast corner where a gravel beach faces Valdes Island.

Observe the tiny unnamed islet-northeast side of Pylades from your kayak only. Attached to Pylades at low tide, this islet is private land. Pylades Island residents are concerned about recreational use and will request anyone landing here to move on.

Three–ha (7 ac) Whaleboat Island is an undeveloped marine park with a shoreline completely lined with sandstone and large boulders that continue up through the scrub and forest. There are no beaches to land on. Overnighters who are willing to sleep under the stars with only space for a single sleeping pad will discover there is room to camp on the northernmost point. Only as a desperate measure would most paddlers choose to go ashore. This island was called Eagle Island prior to becoming a park in 1981.

There are several summer cottages along the eastern shore of Ruxton Island. Seals typically haul out on the drying reefs between Ruxton and De Courcy Islands.

~

Quiet south-facing cove, Pirate's Cove Marine Park. Photo: Andrew Madding.

Pirate's Cove Marine Park

Pirate's Cove, named "Gospel Cove" by the Aquarians, is now a 30 ha (76 ac) marine park. There are two coves in the park, and by far the most popular with recreation boaters is the "U"–shaped bay facing the northwest. Paddlers will likely prefer landing in the lesser–used south–facing cove. From this beach, trails lead to designated campsites. There is a water pump above the cove. A user fee is charged for overnight stays here. Remember this is a pack–in, pack–out park—there are no waste disposal facilities.

~

Paddle the shallow pass between the long, narrow islet and the mid–eastern shore of De Courcy Island. This rich intertidal area is abundant with clams and oysters—but of greater note is the large number of sand dollars, more than I've seen anywhere in the Gulf Islands.

Continue paddling the cottage–lined eastern shore of De Courcy, and return to Cedar–By–The–Sea by paddling between Link and De Courcy Islands. Otherwise, portage across the gravel bar between Link and Mudge Islands and return to the Cedar–by–the–Sea launch.

Two routes easily extend this trip. Cross Pylades Channel to join up to trip 23, Valdes Island, or return to the Cedar–By–The–Sea launch via trip 22, False and Dodd Narrows.

22 False Narrows and Dodd Narrows

Difficulty Intermediate conditions – moderate risk
Distance 4 nmi round trip
Duration Day trip
Charts 3443, Thetis Island to Nanaimo (1:40,000)
Tides Reference Port: Point Atkinson
Secondary Port: Nanaimo
Currents Reference Station: Dodd Narrows
Secondary Station: False Narrows
Camping No camping
Land Jurisdictions Not applicable

An impressive "conveyor belt" of water, Dodd Narrows has tidal streams reaching 10 knots. View the tumultuous, full–flood waters as they disgorge into Northumberland Channel from the bluffs on Mudge Island. In the winter months, paddle the waters fronting the Harmac mill to view the dozens of sea lions that over–winter here. Look for the huge pinnipeds hauled out on the log booms or rafting up in the water.

Safety Considerations

The 10 knot currents in Dodd Narrows and the currents that run about half that speed in False Narrows absolutely demand consideration. Schedule passing through Dodd Narrows at slack only, and pass through False Narrows close to slack.

Expect turbulent water not only in the channels, but also in areas where tidal streams spill into Northumberland and Pylades Channels. Steep waves are especially common when the flood waters from Dodd Narrows disgorge into Northumberland Channel. Approach this area with caution.

Except for offshore breezes and occasional southeasters, summer winds in this area are calm.

This route is not recommended for inexperienced paddlers.

Getting There and Launching

Refer to the Cedar–by–the–Sea launch described in the launch section for trip 21, The De Courcy Group.

The Route

From the Cedar–by–the–Sea launch head toward Round Island and then crossing from Round Island to the north end of Link Island (1 nmi). As currents in the northern sections of Stuart Channel are influenced by flows in Dodd Narrows, paddlers can expect increased tidal flows in this area. Watch for eddylines and whorls off south and east sides of Round Island during a strong ebb.

Link and Mudge Islands are actually joined by an extensive pebble beach (tombolo). Lift kayaks and gear across the tombolo to gain the quickest access to False Narrows. Because currents in False Narrows reach up to 4.5 knots, schedule paddling through so that route direction and current are not at odds. Better still, go through with a slower–moving flood tide (within an approximate hour of slack) and take advantage of the gentler–moving east–to–west flow.

Both Mudge and Gabriola Islands' shores are lined with summer cottages and permanent residences. Few areas look interesting enough to justify landing except for one area known locally as "The Brickyard." Look for a beach cobbled with bricks on Gabriola's shore. The remaining bricks, stamped with "Dominion," are the only remnants of a factory that operated here from 1895 to 1952.

The Harmac mill smokestacks that welcome paddlers to Northumberland Channel are optimistically described as being visible for miles and therefore providing a convenient indication of wind direction, as well as many brilliant sunsets. (Wolferstan)

Occasional visitors to Northumberland Channel are the California sea lions. When they overwinter in this area their loud honking barks can be heard for miles. Typically they haul out on log booms adjacent to the mill or simply raft up. Usual rafting posture is with flippers extended out of the water, likely to minimize heat loss. Paddlers choosing to cross over for a close–up view of these large pinnipeds should favour the Gabriola shore and cross to Harmac well away from Dodd Narrows.

Approach Dodd Narrows from the tip of Mudge Island, and while waiting for slack, climb the adjacent rock bluffs for lofty views of the gap once called Nanaimo Rapids. At full flood, this gorge of water runs up to 10 knots. It is totally impassable by sea–kayak an hour before slack. Half an hour later, it begins to look promising. Finally, fifteen minutes prior to slack, the narrows are passable, but even then, enter the passage with some caution. You may discover a tug with several booms in tow heralding this moment as his own to pass through.

Along the 1.5 nmi return stretch to Cedar–By–The–Sea, few places permit or inspire landing. Pull out at the Fawcett Road ramp.

23 Valdes Island – Valdes, Gabriola, Galiano and the Flat Top Islands

Difficulty Intermediate conditions – moderate risk
Distance 15 nmi round trip
Duration 2 – 3 days
Charts 3343 – Thetis Island to Nanaimo (1 40,000)
Tides Reference Port: Fulford Harbour
Secondary Ports: Degnen Bay and Porlier Pass
Reference Port: Point Atkinson
Secondary Ports: Silva Bay, Dionisio Point and Valdes Island
Currents Reference Stations: Gabriola Passage and Porlier Pass
Camping Blackberry Point, Dionisio Point Provincial Park, Wakes Cove Marine Park
Land Jurisdictions BC Parks – Dionisio Point Park, Wakes Cove Marine Park
Indian Reserve – several sites on Valdes Island

Valdes Island is almost completely uninhabited. Paddle the western shore to one of the most beautiful camp areas in all the Gulf Islands, Blackberry Point. Explore the island's interior by following any one of a number of old logging roads. Paddle along sandstone cliffs to take in the convoluted shapes and intricate patterns carved by the sea. Don't miss a stopover at Degnen Bay and Gabriola's petroglyphs. Spend time on the shores Gabriola Passage in the newest of the province's Marine Parks, Wakes Cove. Finally, paddle the exposed shores on the east side of Valdes where the Strait of Georgia and the distant Coast Mountains provide a spectacular backdrop. Porlier Pass heralds one of the best marine park set–ups for kayakers, Galiano's Dionisio Point Provincial Park.

Paddling Considerations

Two major passes, Porlier Pass at the south end of Valdes and Gabriola Passage at the north end, have tidal streams reaching up to 9 knots. It is therefore necessary that paddlers schedule paddling through them close to slack.

Currents are otherwise minimal, although paddlers may choose to schedule paddling north with a flood and south with an ebb.

Waters on the outside of Valdes Island and around the Flat Top Islands are exposed to prevailing northwest winds in Strait of Georgia. Listen to wind predictions prior to paddling this stretch.

Waters on the inside of Valdes are sheltered from most winds,

Naming of Valdes Island

Valdes Island was named by Captain George Richards of *H.M.S Plumper* in 1859 after Captain Cayetano Valdes of the schooner *Mexicana*, 1792. Valdes commanded the 84-gun *Neptuno* at Trafalgar. She was captured but was wrecked in the storm which followed the battle.

but open to occasional southerly squalls blowing up Trincomali and Pylades Channels.

Given the overall distances, the speed of the currents in the narrow passes and the exposure to winds along the outside of Valdes, this route is not recommended for inexperienced paddlers.

Getting There and Launching
Launch from Degnen or Silva Bay on Gabriola Island or from North Galiano's Spanish Hills Store.

To access Gabriola Island's Degnen Bay launch, take Highway 1 north from Victoria to Nanaimo, then follow signs to Nanaimo's Gabriola ferry terminal. (Paddlers coming from Nanaimo or from Nanaimo's Departure Bay terminal, follow signs to the centre of Nanaimo and then to the Gabriola Island ferry.) The Gabriola ferry docks at Descanso Bay on Gabriola Island. From the terminal, follow South Road to Degnen Bay Road, then turn right and follow Degnen Bay Road to its seaward terminus. Launch from the government wharf or from the adjacent beach, leaving vehicles parked along Degnen Bay Road. Allow an hour and a half to drive from Victoria to Nanaimo, plus twenty minutes to drive from Descanso Bay to the Degnen Bay launch.

To Access Gabriola Island's Silva Bay launch follow the directions in the previous paragraph to Degnen Bay Road. Instead of turning right onto Degnen Bay Road follow South Road another couple of kilometers to the well signed Silva Bay Resort and Marina, 3383 South Road. The launch is accessed adjacent to the marina

pub. You can leave your vehicle in the marina parking lot.

Launching from Galiano Island is most convenient for paddlers coming from the mainland, because travelling to Galiano from Tsawwassen requires only one ferry sailing. To access this launch, board a Galiano–bound ferry at either Tsawwassen or Swartz Bay. Ferries dock at Galiano Island's Sturdies Bay. Leave the ferry terminal, and follow Sturdies Bay Road to Porlier Pass Road, then turn right and follow Porlier Pass Road almost the entire length of Galiano Island. Launch from the government wharf at North Galiano, adjacent to the now–closed Spanish Hills Store. Refer to map on page 124.

The Route
The route described here assumes a launch from Galiano and a circumnavigation of Valdes Island in a clockwise direction. Although this route is described as a complete circumnavigation of Valdes, paddlers may choose to do only one or two of the three sections described: Valdes Island – West Side, Gabriola Passage and the Flat Tops or Valdes Island – East Side. The launches support paddling this route in its entirety or in sections.

Valdes Island – West Side
Launch from the government wharf on the north end of Galiano Island and head toward Porlier Pass. As tidal streams reach up to 9 knots in the pass, swing well out from the entrance to avoid being swept into the channel. Navigate toward Cardale Point on the south end of Valdes Island.

Approaching Blackberry Point. Photo: Bob Davidson.

Until the beginning of this century, a large native population inhabited the southern shores of Valdes, living in one of three permanent villages. The largest village, Laysken, spread north and south of Shingle Point and had as many as ten houses and a population of two hundred. A smaller village at Cardale Point had five houses and a total population of one hundred. The smallest site included three or four houses stretching from Cayento Point to Vernaci Point (Rozen). The villages were abandoned when populations became so depleted that the remaining few inhabitants had to join up with related bands.

Paddlers requesting permission to camp on any of the reserve lands on Valdes are asked to contact the Lyackson Band Office in Chemainus. Up until recently, permission could be obtained by speaking directly to natives living on Shingle Point; however, this handful of inhabitants has relocated to Vancouver Island. (See "Reserve Lands" in the introduction .)

Blackberry Point
Blackberry Point is Crown land and a stopover haven. Immediately impressive is the extensive sand beach surrounding the point. Equally attractive is the meadow that provides level ground for tenting. However Blackberry is continually subject to change. Weyerhaeuser has timber rights to the forests here. The Sea Kayak As-

sociation of BC had an agreement with Weyerhaeuser that in the least provided opportunity for dialogue and at best allowed a group of volunteer paddlers to maintain the quality of the campsite and put in composting toilets. As of 2004 those agreements had lapsed and Weyerhaeuser was gearing up to log once again. It appears that Blackberry lands will once again support logging operations. Assuming the arbutus–sheltered shoreline remains intact camping opportunities will remain. As this whole area faces west, the hours of sunlight are long and views of sunsets are spectacular.

The cliffs that surround Blackberry Point are set farther back than their close–to–shore counterparts on north Valdes, but are equally spectacular as they rise up over 150 m (500 ft). Yes, it is possible to climb to the top of the cliffs, but from a cove about 0.5 nmi north of Blackberry Point. The cove, obviously used as a landing for past logging, marks the beginning of the steep ascent. Land on the pebble beach and start out using the old roadway, then break off in a easterly direction toward Mexicana Hill. Although no single trail leads to the destination, the route becomes obvious—simply head upward toward the cliff tops. Those who question whether or not the vertical climb is worth the effort will put aside doubt as views from 150 m (500 ft) begin to appear. The final vista includes all the islands

Eroded sandstone cliffs, northwest shore of Valdes Island. Photo: Bob Davidson.

from Galiano to Gabriola. Pause for awhile. Twenty eagles were counted soaring above the cliffs during an early May visit. Look across Pylades Channel to Thetis Island. According to native legend, an underground tunnel connects Thetis to Valdes Island. Young men reportedly descended into a cavern on Mexicana Hill and walked 3 mi under the sea to the exit on Thetis Island's Moore Hill in an act that was supposed to be part of a puberty ritual.

Continue along the western shore of Valdes to about midway along the reserve shoreline. Here is an obvious indentation, easily pinpointed using the chart, where, during all but the dry months, a fresh water creek empties into the sea. Known locally as Hole in the Wall you can beach your kayak and climb the nearby knoll to a large open meadow. Meadowlands and views over Pylades Channel will tempt many to stay and camp. However, permission to stay overnight must be obtained beforehand from the Lyackson Band Office in Chemainus. (See the Introduction for contact numbers.)

Valdes Island was logged in the 1950s, and as a result, the entire island is crisscrossed by a network of overgrown roadways. Pull out onto rock ledges located at the base of any number of old landings that, although covered with undergrowth, are still visible. Quickly link up with old byways that lead to the interior, passing through the salal, heading up along rock bluffs and entering evergreen and arbutus forests. Roads frequently break into open areas where rusting drums and thick chain are all that remain of past logging.

Sandstone galleries on the north end of Valdes are simply the most magnificent of the many in the Gulf Islands. Steep cliffs rise abruptly to over 60 m (200 ft) and are intricately carved by wave erosion. The imagination is inspired as the convoluted shapes take on the look of sea serpents, huge beehives and mushroom–shaped clouds. Consider paddling along these cliff faces at low tide for an added treat. The displays of intertidal life at this time are fantastic! In the upper reaches, blue mussels and acorn barnacles firmly attach themselves to the vertical rocks. A middle zone is coloured with congregations of green anemone, cream–coloured thatched barnacles, purple stars, white tube worms and red and brown crab. Below, the white plumose anemone sweep the plankton–rich water for food, and the soft–skinned leather star seek the next victim.

Gabriola Passage and the Flat Tops

Dibuxante Point heralds the southwest entrance to Gabriola Passage. The passage is the smallest of the three major passes leading into the Gulf Islands and has currents reaching up to 8 knots. These strong tidal flows are in large part responsible for the abundance and diversity of marine life found here. Over 200 species of algae, sponges, mollusks, sea stars, crustaceans, fishes and marine mammals inhabit this area. Paddlers will want to time their passage close to slack. Expect the fastest–moving water between Cordero Point and Jan Josef Point. Be aware too that many other vessels converge on this pass near slack. Tugs with full booms

Weldwood Site

Two amateur archaeologists, Ted and Mary Bentley, recorded and produced rubbings of various petroglyphs on Gabriola Island, but in 1976 they discovered the island's most significant site.

Many island residents knew of the site location due to its distinct setting—a natural clearing surrounded by forest—but none dreamed that hidden under the thin layer of grass and moss were so many ancient carvings. One Gabriola pioneer remembers playing on the site as a child while others remember logging operations during World War II. (Scratch marks from steel treads are still visible.)

When the Bentleys made their discovery, the property was owned by Weldwood of Canada. Weldwood offered support in protecting the area when informed of the significant petroglyphs on its land by deeding the land to the Crown. The site is now protected by the province.

By 1980 over fifty petroglyphs were recorded. Among the figures represented are faces, weird humanoids, bird–like creatures, fish and mythical sea creatures, as well as geometric designs such as a foot, eyes, concentric circles, "S" shapes, curves and lines (Bentley).

What purpose did the site serve to ancient peoples? Since such an aura of mystery and seclusion surrounds this forest opening, some speculate it may have been used as a sacred centre. How old is the site? The age of petroglyphs is not easily determined. One figure shows a depression possibly representing a labret carved beneath a humanoid's mouth. This "T"–shaped bone, worn by females on the lower lip, was a beautifying device used from 500 B.C. to about 500 A.D. Possibly these carvings were executed about this time.

The precise meaning and exact age of these petroglyphs are not known, yet these unanswered questions only add to the mystery and inspire our imaginations.

Paddlers searching for detailed information on these petroglyphs should have a look at *Gabriola: Petroglyph Island*, by Ted and Mary Bentley.

---

labour through the narrows, as does every imaginable pleasure craft that uses this shortcut from the Gulf Islands to Vancouver.

From Dibuxante Point paddlers may choose one of two options to get through Gabriola Passage. The first option follows Gabriola Island shores providing paddlers access to Degnen Bay, Drumbeg Park and eventually Silva Bay and the Flat Top Islands. The second option follows Valdes Island shores providing access to Wakes Cove Marine Park.

Paddlers choosing the first option will cross Gabriola Passage from Dibuxante Point to Degnen Bay. Although the worst flows in passage occur farther to the east, expect eddylines, fast–moving water and turbulence in this part of the channel, especially in the shallows that surround the light. Avoid difficult–to–handle conditions by crossing close to slack.

Degnen Bay

Although Degnen Bay has no facilities, this secluded bay has a delightful West Coast charm all of its own. Paddle past the wharf toward the head of the bay to view the "killer whale" petroglyph. The well known petroglyph is located about 5 m (16 ft.) below the high tide line, carved into a sloping sandstone ledge.

There is another petroglyph site on Gabriola that must not be missed. It is called the "Weldwood Site." A hike is required, so pull kayaks up high on the beach near the government wharf (anticipate an hour–long absence from the boats). Follow the gravel road from the wharf to its intersection with South Road. Turn left. Just past the intersection with Thompson Road, look for the United Church. Follow the church's driveway up to the parking area, look to the right for a forest trail. Within several hundred metres, the path makes a left turn toward a very visible clearing (two stone boulders mark the entrance). This remarkable opening in the forest contains sandstone slabs with more than fifty carved petroglyphs. The largest of the petroglyphs is thought to represent a mythical sea serpent.

~

Continue following the Gabriola Island side of Gabriola Passage to the shores of Drumbeg Provincial Park. Although camping is not permitted, this park is worth a stopover. From the obvious beach access wander through the 20 ha (50 ac) of forest, or walk from the beach to a beautiful meadow that looks out over the water.

Gabriola's Silva Bay is a major marine centre. Powerboats and sailboats move in and out of the port, taking full advantage of fuel, repair, lodging and moorage facilities. All shores that line the bay are crowded with commercial facilities, private floats and a Royal Vancouver Yacht Club outstation. Of greatest interest to paddlers are a couple of grocery stores, a marine pub and a restaurant.

Flat Top Islands

If you want seclusion, head to the quieter ambience of the Flat Top Islands. Paddlers looking for a day trip in the Flat Tops can put in at the Silva Bay Resort and Marina. Cars can be left in the marina's parking lot.

The Flat Top Islands present both sheltered channels and exposed stretches of coast. Homes are sparse, but "private" signs are not. If paddlers don't mind being confined to their kayak or below high tide line on the beaches, this delightful archipelago offers some excellent touring.

Don't miss windswept Carlos Island. A single arbutus grows horizontally, revealing the exposed nature of this tiny islet. You can go ashore as this is crown land. In April, look for pockets of yellow monkey–flowers between the boulders and at any time of year enjoy the intricately sculpted sandstone on its northern shore.

In an earlier guide book I described camping on the larger of two unnamed islets between Saturnina and Bath Islands. I recommend limiting a visit to this little islet to daytime for two reasons. The first is that at high tide steep–sided shores make landings difficult. The second is the formation of nearby Wakes Cove Marine Park. At low tide, landings are easy as this islet is joined to Saturnina by a gravel beach. The beach serves as an excellent lunch stop.

Sandstone formations, unnamed islet adjacent tp Saturnia Island. Photo: Mary Ann Snowden.

At this point you can end the trip by returning to the launch at either Degnen or Silva Bay or carry on with the remaining Valdes Island trip.

Wakes Cove

Paddlers who chose the second of the Gabriola Passage route options will paddle along the Valdes Island side of the passage providing access to the newest park within the BC Marine Park system, Wakes Cove. British Navy Captain Arden Wake was granted the land now within the park in 1876. He and his son Baldwin, developed the farm still in evidence here. At the time of Baldwin's death in 1904 the property was transferred to his wife Amelia who subsequently passed the property to long–time family friends, the Wardills. The property remained in the Wardill family until they sold the property to the province for park purposes in 2002. Wakes Cove Marine Park was established in June of that year.

Parks has installed a float and ramp to facilitate access to the 200 hectare (490 acre) park at the head of Wakes Cove, located on Gabriola Passage on the inside of Cordero Point. Paddlers should have no trouble discerning the difference between this public float and an adjacent private pier owned by the Wardill Family (signed Gin Palace Yacht Club). From the park's ramp follow the old logging road that bears left to gain access to the old homestead. Open meadows, numerous farm buildings, rail fencing and a rustic homestead add to the idyllic appeal of this once active sheep farm.

At the time of this writing (2003) there was no designated camp loca-

tion at Wakes Cove. However, BC Parks had plans underway to establish a wilderness campsite at Dogfish Bay. The site will be accessed from the Strait of Georgia side of Wakes Cove from a beach located on the inside and south of Kendrick Island. Development plans for the park include toilets, a covered picnic area, an information kiosk and a kayak storage rack. South and west of this site was land purchased by Brother XII in the 1920s. It was here that he reportedly built his "House of Mystery."

Valdes Island – East Side

Kayakers paddling the east side of Valdes should consider that upon leaving Gabriola Passage and the nearby Flat Tops they are entering into the exposed waters within the Strait of Georgia. Most of the shoreline on the east side of Valdes Island is rocky, and there are few suitable landings. Check wind forecasts for the Strait of Georgia prior to paddling this stretch of coast.

One of the few sand beaches is in an unnamed cove about halfway along the reserve area, where you can land on a sandy beach. There is a freshwater stream nearby, but don't depend on it as a source of water, because during the summer, flows taper off. It is possible to camp here, but once again, permission to use these reserve lands as with those on the western side of Valdes must be obtained prior to landing.

Exposed rocky coast continues from here to Detwiller Point. Most of the homes on Valdes Island are found between Detwiller and Shah Points. Since there are no ferries to Valdes, these homes are accessible by boat only. A delightful little cove behind Shah Point is worth exploring. An arbutus–lined meadow and magnificent views to distant Coast Mountains add to the appeal of this stopover. Offshore are the Canoe Islets, home to hundreds of glaucous–winged gulls. These islets are designated within the province's ecological reserve system and are closed to the public in order to protect nesting birds. California and Steller sea lions are known to use these bare rocks as a winter haul–out.

Porlier Pass has tidal streams reaching 9 knots, and although the bays offer some protection from the faster–moving water, you will encounter huge tide rips, eddies and standing waves out in the rock–congested pass. Use the Tide and Current Tables to determine slack water. Unpredictable eddies and huge rips are also a problem in the 1–mi–long crossing from Valdes to Dionisio Point. Avoid this crossing, except close to slack water.

Dionisio Point Provincial Park

Dionisio Point Provincial Park is a "must do." These 147 ha (360 ac) overlooking Porlier Pass were only recently granted park status. Driftwood shacks used to line these shores, built by loggers and coal miners who used them while fishing in Porlier Pass. Several of the cabins were almost fifty years old when a second occupation began in the early 1970s by those seeking an alternative West Coast lifestyle. Eventually all buildings were razed in an attempt to open up the area for public use. For the next decade recreational

vehicles pulled up, having travelled a rough four–wheel–drive road to gain access. Unfortunately the bay was subsequently subject to overcrowding and some abuse of the natural environ– ment. In the early 1990s Dionisio Point Provincial Park was formed.

Stunningly picturesque is sand–fringed Coon Bay, joined by a narrow isthmus to arbutus–studded Dionisio Point and curving around to Steven's Point. Coon Bay and the adjacent sandstone–ledged bay dry at low tide, providing opportunity to explore the diverse intertidal life associated with these different habitats. Inland, kilometres of interpretive trails run through the understorey of Douglas fir, hemlock and cedar forests. Pathways that parallel the shores of the Strait of Georgia and Porlier Pass spill onto open headlands providing unimpaired views across the strait to the mainland's Coast Mountains and Valdes Island. In positive evidence is BC Parks' attempt to revegetate fragile areas. Steven's and Dionisio Points both show signs of a return to original vegetation now that camping is restricted to designated sites.

The development of Dionisio is, from this kayaker's perspective, BC Marine Parks at its best. The park was once accessible to vehicles. However a controversial subdivision development led to the road closure in mid 90s. The park is now accessed by cyclists, day users, walk–in campers and paddlers only. Most attractive to kayakers is a section of the park developed specifically for paddlers. It is water accessed only and is located along Galiano's eastern shore. Paddle past Coon Bay, and within 500 metres

Paddling through Porlier Pass at slack tide. Photo: Rene Zich.

a BC Marine Parks portal sign comes into view. Land on the gently sloping sandstone ledges, and lift kayaks and gear up a convenient, Parks–constructed stairway. Immediately accessible are 15 designated sites, unobtrusively developed, forest bordered, complete with evergreen–framed water views. Additional facilities include pit toilets, a self–registration vault that collects a reasonable per person fee and a Parks information shelter. Conveniently constructed close to the stairway, is a rack providing empty kayaks above–tide storage. A ten–minute hike along the interpretive trail leads back to Coon Bay where a freshwater pump and a well–organized system for recyclables are situated. Otherwise, this is a pack–in, pack–out set–up. Understandably, a strict "No Fires" regulation is enforced here.

Reluctantly, paddlers will leave Dionisio to return to the North Galiano launch. Enter Porlier Pass at slack to safely paddle Galiano's northern shoreline. The two lighthouses on Race and Virago Points have guided vessels through the pass for nearly a century. Both are now automated. The dilapidated boardwalk and quaint shingle–sided houses on Lighthouse Bay are on private reserve land. The natives live closer to Acala Point and do grant access to those who ask permission. Paddle the final stretch from Acala Point following the northwest shore of Galiano to return to the government wharf launch.

Bibliography

Barman, Jean; *The Worth of an Everyday Woman, Maria Mahoi and Her Two Families*, (Professor, Department Educational Studies, University of British Columbia)

Bentley, Ted and Mary; *Gabriola: Petroglyph Island*; Sono Nis Press; revised, 1998.

Chettleburg, Peter; *An Explorers Guide to the Marine Parks of British Columbia*; Heritage House, 1985.

Gould, G.; *Genoa Bay Reckonings*; Lambrecht Publications; Duncan, 1981.

Government of Canada; *Sea Kayaking Safety Guide*; 1999.

Hill, Beth and Ray; *Indian Petroglyphs of the Pacific Northwest*; Hancock House, 1974.

McBride, Laurie; *Orca Pass Gains Momentum*; Wave Length Magazine; August/September, 2003.

Murray, Peter; *Homesteads and Snug Harbours*; Horsdal and Schubert; Ganges, 1991

Oliphant, John; *Brother Twelve: The Incredible Story of Canada's False Prophet*; McClelland and Stewart, 1992.

Pojar and McKinnon; *Plants of Coastal British Columbia*; Lone Pine, 1994.

Ricketts and Calvin; *Between Pacific Tides*; 4th ed., revised by Ricketts; Stanford University Press; 1968.

Rozen, David; *Permanent Winter Villages and Resource Utilization of the Indian People on Valdez, Galiano and Thetis Island Areas of the Gulf Islands*; Report submitted to the Heritage Conservation Branch of BC, 1978.

Starkin, Ed; *A BC Leper Colony in Raincoast Chronicles: The First Five*; Harbour Publishing, 1976.

Wolferstan, Bill; *Cruising Guide to British Columbia, Volume 1, Gulf Islands and Vancouver Island From Sooke to Courtney*; Whitecap Books, 1995.

Additional Reading

Alderson, Doug; *Sea Kayak Around Vancouver Island*: Rocky Mountain Books, 2004

Alderson and Pardy; *Sea Kayaker Magazine's Handbook of Safety and Rescue*; Ragged Mountain Press, 2003.

Backlund and Grey; *Kayaking Vancouver Island: Great Trips From Port Hardy to Victoria*; Harbour Publishing, 2003.

Baron and Acorn; *Birds of the Pacific Northwest*; Lone Pine, 1997.

Burch, David; F*undamentals of Kayak Navigation*; Globe Pequot Press, 1999.

Butler, Rob; *The Great Blue Heron*; UBC Press, 1997.

Duehl, Lois; *Pacific Seaweeds*; Harbour Publishing; 2001.

Ford, Ellis and Balcomb; *Killer Whales: The Natural History and Genealogy of Orincas Orcain British Columbia and Washington State*; 2000.

Harbo, Rick; Pacific Reef and Shore: *A Guide to Northwest Marine Life;* Harbour Publishing, 2003.

Kahn, Charles; *Hiking the Gulf Islands: A Recreation Guide to BC's Enchanted Isles*; Harbour Publishing, 2004.

Koppel, *Tom; Kanaka, the Untold Story of Hawaiian Pioneers in British Columbia and the Pacific Northwest*; Whitecap Books, 1995.

McGee, Peter; *Kayak Routes of the Pacific Northwest*; Greystone Books, 2004.

Sheldon, Ian; *Seashore of British Columbia*; Lone Pine, 1998.

Snively, Gloria; *Exploring the Seashore in British Columbia, Washington and Oregon: A Guide to Shorebirds and Intertidal Plants and Animals*; Gordon Soules, 1999.

Contact Information

Marine Weather
- Vancouver 604-664-9010 Victoria 250-363-6880 or 250-363-6492
- www.weatheroffice.ec.gc.ca

Marine Charts and Canadian Tide Tables
- Volume 5: Juan de Fuca Strait and Strait of Georgia Tide and Current Tables; Canadian Hydrographic Services, annual publication
- www.charts.gc.ca

Canadian Coastguard
- Coast Guard Marine Emergency: 1-800-567-5111 or 1-800-661-9202
- Boating Safety Information: www.boatingsafety.gc.ca or 1-800-267-6687

Parks
- Parks Canada – Gulf Islands National Park Reserve www.gulfislands@pc.gc.ca
- BC Parks and BC Marine Parks www.bcparks.ca

Ferries
- BC Ferries www.bcferries.bc.ca
  Reservations: 1-888-724-5223 or out of province call 604-444-2890
- Washington State Ferries www.wsdot.wa.gov/ferries/ or call 1-888-808-7977
- Coho Ferry www.cohoferry.com or call Blackball Transport 250-386-2202

Kayak Specialty Shops, Tour Companies and Rentals
- Wave Length Magazine www.WaveLengthMagazine.com

Canadian Fisheries and Oceans Regulations and Guidelines
- Fishing Regulations www.pac.dfo-mpo.gc.ca.
- Marine Mammal Viewing Guidelines www-comm.pac.dfo-mpo.gc.ca/pages/MarineMammals/view_e.htm

Indian Reserve Lands – Native Bands
- Lyackson Band, Ladysmith, B.C. (Reserves on Valdez Island) 250-246-5019
- Penalukut Band, Kuper Island (Tent Island Reserve) 250-246-2321
- Tsawout Band, Saanichton (Saturna Island- Fiddler's Cove Reserve) 250-652-9101
- Songhees Band, Victoria (Chatham and Discovery Island Reserve Lands) 250-386-1043
- Becher Bay Band, Sooke (Becher Bay Reserve Lands) 250-478-3535

Marine Conservation – see page 28

Index

In Case Of Emergency

- VHF Radio – Frequency 156.8 MHhz channel 16. Signal Maday (3 times) indicating your name and position and the type of assistance you require.

- Distress Flares – flares burn for several seconds to a minute and can be seen for several miles.

- Distress Signal – 3 signals at intervals of about one minute – a whistle or a flashlight.

- Cellular – dial *16

- Coast Guard Marine Emergency 1-800-567-5111 or 1-800-661-9202